A Small Business Owner (SE

The SBO:
PLANNING FOR PITFALLS

By Nelson L. Marsh

Edited By:
G.E. Marsh

a Hobby Fuzion LLC Imprint

SBO: Planning For Pitfalls

Published in the United Sates by Hobby Fuzion LLC

Printed in the United States of America

First Printing, 2017

ISBN 978-0-9996385-0-7

eBook ISBN 978-0-9996385-1-4

10 9 8 7 6 5 4 3 2 1

CONTENTS

READ THIS FIRST

How to use this book.

This book is intended to familiarize Small Business Owners (SBO) with the common Business Pitfalls they will need to face and overcome in the course of starting up and running their own small business. In many of the chapters the reader will find business exercises to work through. It is highly encouraged that the small business owner takes the time to go through each exercise thoroughly and do so multiple times so the reader can identify the major potential pitfalls of their business venture before committing considerable time and resources.

This book is not intended to teach the reader how to prepare an industry standard formal business plan or lay out step by step every facet of your new business. For formal business plan preparation, the reader is encouraged to refer to readily available Business Planning books, online business planning software, tutorials, or professional business classes.

This book has been prepared with a deliberate effort to render legally complex financial language into lay or common use terms whenever possible. Technically and legally complex business language is contained however by necessity, but this is unavoidable if you want to understand the SBO startup process.

A short glossary of terms is included to aid you in recognition of official terms or unique definitions found within this work.

For legal compliance issues, always seek out any law or code term definitions from their originating sources (Example: For the latest interpretation of Internal Revenue Service terms and definitions refer to the IRS website).

Finally when reading, remember to never take business personally and that the answer to any unasked question will always be NO.

The SBO:

PLANNING FOR PITFALLS

CHAPTER
-1-

"Keep thy shop, and thy shop will keep thee."

-Benjamin Franklin

Small Business Owners (SBO) have long constituted the capital lifeblood of the American economy and it is fair to say this is true for many nations throughout history, past and present.

To begin, we begin with the foundation of understanding what a business is.

At its most basic, a business is a legal entity formed by an individual (or group in some type of partnership such as a corporation – much more on the type of business later) who begins with an idea for offering a product or service they intend to provide in order to receive something of value, usually money or some other goods or services of value, in order to meet specific business goals.

The scope of small business runs the entire spectrum of possibilities, whether talking about large corporations or a single owner-operated company, from brick and mortar stores to internet based web presence only locations.

Yet, for every 1975 Pet Rock® small business success story, there are multitudes of failed business ventures.

Why?

As you can imagine there are many, many answers to that deceptively simple question, and through the course of the following chapters we will explore how to identify and attempt to avoid the major pitfalls made by SBO through a deliberate planning process.

Unfortunately experience has shown that one of the most basic reasons a business fails is that while many new small business owners come into the business world with a fiery enthusiasm to bring their product or service to market, they find the path to success challenging or nearly impossible because they lack even the most basic business working knowledge afforded by a college or university business degree.

What does that really mean in terms of starting or operating a small business?

Without deliberate planning, a business may end before it starts.

Lack of knowledge is one of many direct paths to failure in business.

Do not understand your market competition? Count on limited success or failure.

Do not understand how taxes or payroll works? Failure and legal issues.

Do not understand how laws work? Failure and legal penalties (possibly jail).

Do not understand the mindset that drives your customers? Failure and money loss.

Do not understand how your business location may impact your product or service? Almost a surefire way to start losing money right away.

Do not understand that marketing and advertising are not the same thing?

Maybe not outright failure, but fairly guaranteeing slow to no business growth.

The old adage that knowledge is power has a great deal of validity in the case of operating a successful small business. Understanding where to acquire business knowledge (a type of resource), and how to apply that knowledge in a business setting (resource management) in order to achieve whatever aim or goal you have set for you business is the first step to avoiding business failure.

The identification of knowledge gaps is critical to successful planning.

What you do not know will kill your business, so where do you find business knowledge?

There are many sources of official and unofficial sources of business knowledge available to you. This can range from informal advice to structured business courses at universities offering various business degrees.

So, is a business degree required to own or operate a business?

No.

A business degree in not required to become a small business owner. Legally what will may require a business permit and other legal documentation however, more on that later.

If a business degree is not needed to own or operate a business, then just what knowledge does a business degree really provide?

A business degree from a college, university, or private school (accredited or not) generally nets specialized knowledge in the basics of business skill sets, such as accounting, economics, finance, human resource management, logistics, marketing, advertising, and many more. Note that most structured business educations will focus on one or more areas of specialization that provide a degree in business administration or business management.

Attending and earning a college or university degree for something other than a business degree is no substitute for a actual business accreditation. It is quite common to achieve an advanced degree in say engineering or medicine and come away with little to no actual business knowledge.

Doctors often experience this problem when they first try their own private practice and are surprised at how much they do not know about running a business. After all, business must be easy compared to the human body right? Sadly, the answer is NO.

Does having a business degree's guarantee a successful business?

That answer is again a resounding NO, but with a catch.

Business is both an art and science.

As an art, timely business decisions may rely more on an SBO's life experience, wisdom, and subjective judgment to successfully capitalize on an emerging business opportunity than any business degree textbook answer might provide. People of all backgrounds and skill levels demonstrate daily that a business degree is not necessary to own or run a business. With minimal effort you should easily find examples of companies started by individuals that date back hundreds of years before schools even offered the first business degree!

The rather unsung glory of being a business owner is that anyone has the potential to run a business regardless of their formal education.

It is also true however, that many SBO's have found that having a business degree has greatly helped prepare them to leverage opportunities and avoid basic management pitfalls because business IS a science as well.

A business degree is far from worthless, as it is the direct result of rigorous scientific study that has come to codify how laws and market behave in countries the world over. Business degrees are offered in multiple specialties entirely because of the deep complexities that exists between the rules governing business behavior and legal restrictions governing that behavior. A business degree offers considerable advantage to an SBO in understanding those complexities to manage business decisions and ensures a rather steep learning curve for those without.

Running a business takes a combination of skills, resources, timing, and the ability to take and manage risk to make the most of any business opportunity. Luck helps, but will only get you so far and should never be relied on as a business plan.

Regardless of whether or not you have a business degree, you will have to work hard at developing a thorough understanding of business practices in order to recognize and categorize the challenges you will face during your company start up period and to make sound business decisions.

No amount of education (regardless of the source) will get your business moving unless you establish achievable goals and develop a deliberate plan outlining how to achieve those goals that also accounts for the avoidance of common business pitfalls.

This is the sort of planning that requires vision.

Enter the Dynamic Visionary

Start with understanding how a passion to become a small business owner mixes with a common sense approach to developing a business vision.

A business passion may originate from many drivers, ranging from the need to pay for basic living conditions to an intense desire to bring some product or service to the world that has never been seen.

Your own Pet Rock® you might say.

Whatever your product or service, you need to view it through the lens of business common sense. Business common sense comes from being able to perceive, understand, and judge those things reasonably expected to be a common understanding to your customers. What they need, want, and expect.

Building a better toothbrush?

You may have a real passion for making the cleanest teeth possible, but common sense tells you no one will buy it unless it is competitively priced or needs to be small enough to fit in someones mouth. This is often the areas that individuals with advanced degrees in other than business make their first mistake, they desire to make a product that in fact may be a solution looking for a problem. Sometimes that works out, mostly it is a good exercise is wasting limited resources.

By balancing your business passion and common sense together, the SBO can begin to operate as a Dynamic Visionary.

A Dynamic Visionary is someone able and willing to see in advance problems and opportunities across a broad spectrum of challenges in order to manage risk and avoid making the most frequent small business mistakes.

This is very much the common sense case of look before you leap mentality.

By harnessing the power of your Dynamic Vision, your small business is empowered with the potential to be a thundering financial success story.

The key word here is 'potential'.

Failure to account and deal with business challenges will snuff out that potential quickly. What is worse is that a competitor may capitalize on an unprotected idea and take that potential for themselves.

The business world is full of challenges that are direct obstacles to your success. You must constantly identify, mitigate, and keep in mind each challenge to be overcome in order for your business to reach its true potential for success. With few exceptions, no one is going to be as involved in making your business a success as you, the owner are.

Within the following chapters you will explore work through the process of developing your company Dynamic Vision by reading through discussion examples and conducting workbook like exercises.

Each chapter introduces a critical business concept that you as a SBO must become intimately familiar with. Each topic listed has been shown to be an area where routine and avoidable mistakes are typically made that make up the common pitfalls that cause new businesses to fail. The pitfall discussions and workbook exercises work together to assist you in developing your own Dynamic Vision that will help you plan for success.

Ensure as you read each chapter that you actually complete any exercises contained and keep the results handy. Trust me, you will need those by the time you get to the end.

Not discouraged yet? Great!

Fire up that passion, you just began your journey on becoming a Small Business Owner (SBO).

NELSON L. MARSH

CHAPTER
-2-

"Remember, you will always fail in business if
you don't try to open your own business"

-Markus Pappa

Remember from the opening paragraph from Chapter 1 referencing the Pet Rock®?

Chances are you have heard of the Pet Rock® no matter your current age. Suffice to say if you have heard of this novelty product (even if you have never actually owned one) it is likely because of its remarkable approach to business through an ultra-successful marketing vision that began as a joke and emerged a marketing legend.

So, here is your first worthwhile exercise assignment. Yes, there will be quite a few in this book, but stick with me for now.

Open your favorite internet search engine to search for "Gary Dahl's Pet Rock®" and read all about the idea for a simple product born from a very simple premise.

Done?

Good, now you have some context to better appreciate the author's assertion that EACH business owner or manager has an innate creativity to brainstorm ideas and visions that result in their own Pet Rock®.

Need proof?

You are starting or are currently running a business - that gives you all the incentive you need to work toward success!

The path to success requires a Small Business Owner (SBO) to develop a firm understanding of the variables that create the business environment in which the SBO intends to operate.

The developer of the Pet Rock® saw the environment was right to turn a joke into a multi-million dollar venture.

But how?

He took his passion for a humorously quirky novelty idea and married it to his advertising experience and then developed and implemented detailed planning to lower his overhead costs as far as possible. This is an excellent example of resource management and gut instinct that came together to create a cultural icon.

Developing the Dynamic Vision

In Chapter 1 the concept of the Dynamic Visionary was introduced and the concept that lack of relevant business knowledge is a key concern that needs to be addressed. Additional common business knowledge areas that you will encounter that often trip up the starting SBO include:

Misunderstanding management of your personal and professional expenses.

Not thoroughly researching your market competitors.

Misunderstanding the differences and applications between marketing and advertising.

Not understanding changes in technology (particularly disruptive technology).

Over or under estimating the impacts of cultural trends on their produced good or service.

A primary goal of establishing your Dynamic Vision for your business is to begin identifying and mitigating what variables you can control. Your ultimate goal with this effort is to set conditions for a more predictable environment in which your business can thrive.

Your Dynamic Vision is created from your balance of business passion and common sense.

For the new SBO, it is easy to get overcome with the passion to get a new idea to market, but fail to understand the business conditions surrounding them. After all, the fun is in the product or service for most, but it is the boring details that will make or break your business.

So how does the SBO really become a Dynamic Visionary and make practical use of this processes?

When you are developing your Dynamic Vision, it will be created within the context of your business passion (your product or service) and grounded through your common sense understanding of the market you are selling it in.

Always keep your dreams to inspire your business, but as an old pilot from back-in the-day, allow me to use a favorite flying analogy:

"Get your head up-and-out of the cockpit, and scan the horizon and beyond"

In lay terms, the SBO needs to not only know what information is going on around them (situational awareness), but also create a clear vision of what success looks like for that particular business.

The SBO as a Dynamic Visionary, works to develop an ongoing understanding of business variables within their market and is able to use that situational awareness to create predictive models that that allow them to best position their small business for long term success. Through this process, a viable business plan is formed that is flexible enough to adapt to the future business conditions that starts to emerge.

Business is dynamic and not static. It has and will continue to change.

Plenty of major companies have fallen prey to decline or bankruptcy based solely on their failure to understand changing market conditions.

Did you read the author bio at the back of the book?

If not, take a few minutes to go back and give it a quick glance (not for my own vanity mind you). It is my intent to let the bio provide you some context to reference for the next few bits of information.

Back to applying the Dynamic Vision.

If there is one process that thirty (30) Active Duty years of service as a military officer and over 25 years of running my own small business has taught me it is the value of:

Backward Planning

Now it is quite possible you have never encountered this term, or at least as it is used in regards toward establishing the success of your business.

Backward Planning is simply the deliberate act of starting from a desired end state and working your way back through time to the beginning of your business service or product start, while noting every key business milestone and resource required to meet the set endstate goal.

Simple right?

Here is a classic example of how backward planning is used in the construction industry.

In the construction industry, backward planning is conducted using the Critical Path Method (CPM) first developed by Morgan R. Walker of DuPont and James E. Kelley Jr. in the late 1950's that enables a Project Manager to understand and calculate all the events or activities that need to happen in a particular sequence to finish a project on time.

For instance, before you put a roof on a building you need walls, and to make walls stand, you need a solid foundation. To backward plan, you lay out the foundation, then build the walls until you get to the endstate of putting the roof on.

This endstate analysis process lets the project manager determine and plan for:

The list of all activities required to complete the project.

The time duration that each activity will take to complete.

The dependencies between the activities (the order required) and resources (materials, personnel, skills sets, equipment, and logistics) needed to complete the project.

Taken together, the project manager is able to determine what paths are the most important to prioritize and complete first (the critical path) to reach the endstate without delays. This method enables the project manger to schedule activities when they are needed so resources use is maximized while providing solid estimates on project completion.

A similar concept to the Critical Path Method is the Program Evaluation and Review Technique (PERT), developed by the U.S. Navy around the same time as CPM for development of the Polaris missile design and construction scheduling.

Nuances aside, the concept of the backward planning process is fully applicable to your business development. As you read this book you may be at the very beginning of your small business start-up venture or be looking for clues as to why you as an SBO may not have quite found success yet.

The great news though is that you DO have a place to start from since you do HAVE an endstate, which is of course to be a successful SBO.

Time to start using that the Backward Planning methodology to begin your first business exercise!

Defining Your Endstate

We will now begin with some practical exercises to help you think through your business. Grab something to take notes on, several blank sheets of paper and some erasable pencils or pens will suffice for now (or a data pad or computer if you prefer).

Start this exercise with a simply defined endstate and run it through the SBO Core Principles. This exercise will cover major concepts that will highlight key information that you will need to flesh out for your company business plan.

As an exercise constraint to make it easier to concentrate on the SBO Core Principles, assume for this exercise that you are operating a new company under the business regulations and laws governing of the United States of America.

Note that while the United States is the example sales market for this business exercise and default location for most of this book, the following SBO Core Principles are largely applicable no matter what country your SBO may operate in, from brick and mortar storefront to virtual online presence.

Hold on, before you write, just what is a SBO Core Principle?

A SBO Core Principle is a key business aspect that you as a SBO need to address in order to identify and mitigate variables impacting your business venture.

Back to making some notes on those blank sheets of paper.

SBO Core Principles

Start with writing your working company name (it does not matter what it is, you can change it later) at the top of the paper with your own name as owner underneath. Then write each of the following SBO Core Principles down in order, answering each SBO Core Principle question before moving on to the next.

SBO Core Principle 1
Draft an Endstate to determine your SBO Goal.

Begin with selecting "making $1 million dollars in a year" as your SBO goal. It is just fine for now to run through this first exercise and you might as well start big right?

When you do this exercise again for your own business to refine your own SBO Goal, always keep in mind that your endstate will change as your business matures.

Having a successful business means you get to keep doing this exercise for the life of your business.

An endstate for an SBO should be something that is achievable and actionable within a clearly defined time-frame.

Setting an endstate of being the top provider in the world in a year for a given product or service may be a laudable goal to reach someday, but starting out it may be shooting for failure rather than success since its unlikely to be achievable without planning or resources in place.

Business success is a goal that should always be clearly in your mind, so breaking larger than life business goals into achievable endstate chunks, such as "making $1 million dollars in a year", gives you a target you can both develop a plan for and have a reasonable degree of actually accomplishing.

Wait, but an endstate should mean the end right?

No.

For an SBO, reaching an endstate only means starting another SBO endstate goal until you decide to end your ownership or legally end your involvement in the business.

So what does that draft endstate look like? Well when you being to refine it, it looks a lot like a SMART objective:

S - Specific

M - Measurable

A - Achievable

R - Realistic

T - Time bound

Let's add to the example endstate to to re-write it slightly:

"My company providing X-service will make $1 million dollars in a year"

Now lets break that down into a SMART format to see if it works.

S – "My company providing X-service..." here you outline that it is your company providing a specific service or product.

M – "will make $1 million dollars..." you have set a goal that you can break down into a measurable target to see if you are successful.

A – Is making $1 million dollars achievable? Is it after taxes or expenses?

As a quick visualization exercise, take your pen or pencil and jot that endstate dollar figure example in United States currency form:

$1,000,000.00

Quite the enticing incentive, clear to understand and well defined as a goal!

But it is reasonably achievable?

For legal products or services, the answer is more than likely yes.

If you already come to the conclusion it is not, then you already have a good indicator that you may need to refine that endstate statement.

For now however, lets assume that making a cool million dollars as the endstate goal is achievable.

R – Is it realistic that your company can make $1 million dollars in a year? Do some quick math, divide the $ million dollar goal by 12 months to see how much you need to make to each month. Now not all (or most) businesses follow a linear progression, but do you think it is realistic to be able to make at least $84,000 (yes, you might as well round the number up) each month?

T – "in a year" clearly sets a target for the time you need to meet your specific goal and helps you in determining how realistic and achievable that goal is by setting you constraints to work in.

Naturally 12 months also matches the typical tax year period for most countries.

The endstate represents the start of a lot of important questions for a SBO to consider.

A lot more.

The SMART format is a starting outline for your endstate goal, but it is only there to help you begin to refine your endstate goal. Most of the SBO Core Principles in fact are point topics designed to help you craft the questions you need to answer to have your business meet your SBO draft endstate.

Example questions to apply to your own endstate goal:

"Does the SBO draft endstate target dollar figure represent your take home income, company profit, or just what is needed to keep the business afloat (overhead costs)?"

"Does the SBO draft endstate account for increases in taxes or product material costs or shipping from year to year?"

"Is the SBO draft endstate flexible enough to be achievable with market forecasts that may change (from regulations or laws or supply chain difficulties) that may result in unexpected increases in overhead costs?"

Seems like the concept of simple just left the room right?

Remember, by using your Dynamic Vision you guide the SBO draft endstate to something actionable and achievable within given resources and a timeframe into something you can craft a solid business plan around. This is an exercise to do over and over again until you are satisfied you know you need to understand your business environment.

So how do you know the endstate you selected is the right endstate?

If your draft endstate is within what your business can reasonably achieve for the chosen time frame you are likely on the right track, but for now it is OK to be a bit ambitious and a little audacious in what your endstate is.

Dreaming big is OK.

Being timid in your business goals may mean never realizing those goals.

Through the SBO Core Principles you will develop an understanding that setting your endstate goal too low is just as perilous as setting your goals too high.

By shooting too for low a business goal, you may be missing out on significant business opportunities that may let a competitor corner a market and drive you out of business because you did not see the need to be prepared to grow ahead of time.

Business is Risk, but Risk can be Managed

The very act of writing down and selecting an endstate as an SBO is an act of risk management.

Proceeding through the rest of the following SBO Core Principles will assist you in identifying areas of potential risk and provide potential mitigation solutions.

Manage risk, but do not be afraid to take necessary risks.

When selecting your endstate goal(s) above all else, DO NOT be discouraged if you come up a lot of Unanswered Questions!

Doing this exercise is entirely meant to cause you to deliberately ask yourself all the questions you may have not even realized needed to be asked.

The process of answering those questions will help prepare you to fill in the blanks that will ultimately shape conditions for running a successful small business with potential to grow.

Take as much time as you can afford when selecting your initial endstate goal(s). Time spent now in identifying potential problems in meeting your endstate goal before you actually start your small business operations, may be the difference between financial success or costly failure.

It bears repeating that this endstate identification exercise is something you will repeat many times throughout your company's operational life.

Each time you are close to achieving a specified endstate goal, start working well in advance on your next endstate vision. The time to conduct deliberate business planning is well before you hit your endstate.

Fort this exercise, the time to start planning the next business endstate goal is a year to six months prior to reaching the goal of "making $1 million dollars in a year".

SBO Core Principle 2
What really is the product or service being provided that will allow you to reach your endstate goal?

Professionally, you need to know what your product actually is, whether it is a product being sold or services being rendered.

Sounds a bit silly, but ask yourself if your product or service is really what you think it is?

Is it legal?

Is it ethical?

Is it harmful?

Is it achievable with the resources you have available?

An idea without the ability to execute it may have value, but maybe only as an idea to sell to a company that can capitalize on it. An idea not acted on at all (read as hoarded), produces nothing.

Now is the time to begin to conduct investigations into the market to look for precedents and mitigating solutions. For instance, rules or laws governing a particular market may require a business license or permit to be obtained before you can sell a particular product legally.

More on this later.

As you work through this activity, you may have just discovered you started with a business idea and not your endstate goal. Now you also need to match the business idea and endstate goal together and see if they are compatible.

Can your business idea realistically generate the endstate goal conditions within the time frame you set? Selling a custom made item is unlikely to net you $1 million dollars a year unless you find a buyer willing to pay that amount!

If you do find that buyer at your asking price, are there more of them to make a realistic business that runs year after year or is it a one-shot venture?

If your business idea and endstate goal seems incompatible, then you may need to adjust either the endstate goal or your particular product or service to something that is achievable together.

If they are compatible, then knowing this will help you answer the challenge as to why should your customer or clients should purchase your particular offerings?

Are you offering the market something never seen before or another variation on a product or service in the vein of building-a-better-mousetrap?

If you are making a variation on an existing product or service, is really an improvement or is it something that the market is already flooded with?

If it is the same as everything else, can you still sell enough of it to meet your endstate goals?

You **DO NOT NEED** to make or sell a new product or service that is wholly original (you could license the rights to manufacture an existing product), there are plenty of business models that we will discuss in future chapters that make use of existing products or services – YOU DO however have to make a viable business from selling that product or service.

Does the world need another paperclip or do the existing ones really do just fine? If you cannot make something that exists or distribute them cheaper than existing business sources you likely need to strongly consider moving on to another business idea. Bottom line to remember is to know what exactly it is your business is selling.

SBO Core Principle 3
Determine from where your small business is providing its goods or services to your customer and why that location is optimized for your business.

Where is your business located?

It is cliche, but a large degree of business success is attributable to:

Location – Location – Location

If number SBO Core Principles 1 and 2 were not so important and revisited so often, SBO Principle 3 would be right at the very top of your list to plan for.

Location is a make or break activity for your business.

You need to be able to answer the following:

If producing some product, what is the cost and transportation process to ship goods to and from the small business location? What about manufacturing materials?

Is the point of sales (where the customer makes the purchase) the same as the place of manufacture or are there additional transportation requirements to a storefront? What about warehousing and does it need to be near shipping lanes, highways, airports, or railways?

If providing some service, what are the transportation costs of going to a client?

How about storage of equipment?

Is there enough parking for a client to come to you?

Is the area your small business operates in free of crime?

If the SBO works from a storefront or office, you need to know where your direct/indirect competition is physically sited.

Is there some legal benefit or cost to doing business at this location (local, state, or country codes, regulations, or laws to consider)?

If just starting out, does a Home Office make sense? History shows us that it works nicely for millions of SBO's, but be mindful that great success could render a home office quickly inadequate through the need to grow.

Now while the internet and globalization has made the whole world a potential competitor, it has also made it easier for you to offer your own product or services in a way that customers can find you. What you need to understand is that even where you may decide to host your website on the internet is a location based decision.

Take the time to learn how different search engines dictate the order on which your company may appear (more on marketing and advertising later) and which server hosting services work the best for your business model. Unless you are selling services, files or information on the internet, you are also likely going to need manufacture and storage space for any physical product (including physical marketing materials).

Deciding where you locate your business directly impacts what resources that it takes to operate at that location and directly relates to how customers find and deal with your business.

Recall that profit is what you make after ALL your expenses are paid. Minimizing the cost of business overhead by locating your business in a manner that does not work against your endstate goal is critical.

Always consider and reconsider what are the things about this location that are ultimately impacting your draft endstate goal?

SBO Core Principle 4
Funding Capitalization. Does your Small Business have a healthy cash flow with a reserve?

What this means is "Do you have enough money to start this business?"

It also means "Where is the funding coming from?" Does the funding stem from personal finances, a partnership venture, investor based, bank loan, or some combination?

Time for another time proven cliche.

It takes money to make money

Do you have enough funding to manufacture your product or equipment to provide a service? Even a consulting service has travel and vehicle costs to consider. How much does each item cost to make and how much can you sell at a time to keep cash flowing?

Do you have enough cash to cover a loss-lead product or service until such time you can make a reasonable profit? How long can you sustain this?

Do you have enough funding to outfit the necessary equipment if providing a service such as lawn care?

If you have product you intend to manufacture you need enough funding to buy raw materials, production equipment, trained personnel as well as space to assemble, test, and box products to ship to a point of sale location.

You will also need funding for registering your company, permits, and other overhead costs before your first sale to a customer. Any country you operate in is also going to get their slice of your gains (perhaps even multiple countries). Consider it just one more cost of doing business.

Note that there is also a difference between available cash and assets that will be discussed in some detail later.

SBO Core Principle 5
Employee Personnel.

Is your endstate goal achievable within the sated time frame considering the number and job specialization employees you have to achieve it?

How many people does it take to directly operate your business?

Can you run your small business operation solo?

How many people can you afford to hire (and train)?

Finding success and the need to grow, are you prepared to hire and pay W-2 Employees and their attendant Federal and State Payroll Taxes?

Per the United States Internal Revenue Service (i.e. the IRS):

"Any Employer who cannot afford to pay personnel and Payroll taxes... cannot afford to even be in business"

Sounds harsh, but it is a true fact of running a business, even a relatively small business.

Personnel management is a particular area that often lands a small business owner in financial and legal difficulties.

You need to know the rules and legal regulations regarding everything from potential unions to equal opportunity laws in your business area.

What sort of work hours must be compensated for?

How big a business do you have to be to provide maternity / paternity administrative leave?

Learn your local business requirements County, City, State, Federal, or country. All locations may have different requirements with serious legal implications beyond just cutting into your profit margins. A good place to start to find out is a local business bureau or state employment office.

In general you can expect that employees in the United States have rights that include:

Work in a safe work environment or if the work is inherently dangerous (such as mixing chemicals) that all necessary safety precautions are enforced.

Work free from discrimination or harassment.

Work free from fear of retaliation (whistle blower laws).

Work for a fair wage and not under duress or forced labor.

Other rights to be aware of in the United States include as a company gets bigger (typically over 15 or more employees) enforcement of Title VII hiring practices, Americans with Disabilities Act, Age Discrimination in Employment Act, Fair Labor Standards Act, and the Family and Medical Leave Act.

Personnel are the key to successfully growing many a small business to a true juggernaut of success. Many of the largest corporations out there started out in the beginning as something much smaller that grew over time with the help of its employees to dominate their marketplace.

Simply put, managing people fairly and legally is an utter business necessity. Forget that necessity and it could end your business straight off, possibly landing you in a heap of debt and legal trouble.

SBO Core Principle 6
Advertising and Marketing.

How is your endstate goal served by advertising and marking?

Do you need to advertise your market or service at all to meet your endstate goals?

How does the market help or hinder your product or service?

Let start on this one by setting the record straight:

Advertising and Marketing are NOT the same thing

Advertising is simply the act of giving the public information about a product or service, usually to great praise, in order to get customers to buy or use the advertised service or product.

Advertising a product or service that was conducted under false pretenses is illegal and unethical.

You need to definitively know prior to advertising your product or service that it is even legal to sell without infringing on someone holding a copyright, trademark, or patent. If you have not studied up on Copyrights and Trademarks, now is the time to look up the basics (refer to the Glossary from some helpful links).

Stay truthful! Be specific in claims that can be backed up legally.

One thing your small business likely does not have a lot of is money to fend off lawsuits from angry customers. Injuries may come from physical injury, mental injury, or perceived injury. Make sure your advertising does not contain falsehoods that can be used against you later in a court.

If your product or services does injure someone in some way, you will need your resources to defend your business and hopefully be able to make equitable restitution without it sinking your business.

Marketing is the act of buying or selling within a market and is the sum total of all the required activities necessary for the seller of a product or service to a buyer.

Recall earlier about needing to know what market you are in when locating your small business?

Where you conduct your trade may be as simple as getting a business permit to sell produce at a local Farmer's Market to requiring you to understand the nuances of trade laws governing the sales and manufacturing regulations for a specific class of items within a global market (such as textiles for example).

Information on markets of all kinds is readily available through a variety of information sources.

You can obtain much of the market information you require for your specific business to operate from your local business bureaus offices that is very likely accessible through authorized government websites accessed from the comfort of your own home.

Do you need an advertising agency or marketing firm assistance?

An advertising agency is used to develop advertisements, develop brand recognition, and generally get the word out about what your company sells to prospective customers.

A marketing firm is useful to analyze a market and how your product or service may be tailored to optimize sales for your company output.

These types of companies may not be cheap, but if your business is to grow to your endstate (including helping to set a new endstate), then you may need consider investing in this sort of company support, particularly in markets that may be foreign to you or where your product is unknown.

SBO Core Principle 7
Understanding Demographics.

The next concept of the market you need to understand is knowing who your customers actually are.

Who is your product or service really for?

Are there enough potential customers within the market to purchase from my company to make the business profitable?

Demographics is the statistical data of a given market population, which may include such information as age, income, education, ethnicity, or other factors that drive the motivation behind the demand side of sales.

The main questions demographics help a small business to answer are "why do people need your product or service?" and "Can they get your product or service somewhere else cheaper and easier?"

Running a small business means knowing and understanding the particular the demographics of the market you intend to sell to. Invest the time to find out who buys, needs, or utilizes your type of product or services in the market areas you intend to sell and how many potential customers there are to buy products or services from your company.

Knowing this information allows you to target specific customers and helps to ensure that you do not over-saturate a market and drive your sales prices down. This information assists you in optimizing your sales output against rival companies by understanding where potential customers needs are not being met. Customers can be very fickle and easily shift their buying power elsewhere, occasionally appearing irrationally so.

Treat every customer as an individual, but study the market demographic in order to reach them.

Be particularly wary of demographic data that chases a specific trend customers have for a product. Trends by their definition are short lived and history is replete with products offered by one time successful companies that time and technology have passed by.

SBO Core Principle 8
"Talkers" or "Doers"

You do not need to ask if you are a Talker or a Doer – by taking up the challenge of starting or running a business means you are a doer!

The question is how does your endstate deal with customers habits that may impact your sales?

For this exercise, practically every client or customer can be classified as either a "Talker" or "Doer".

Talkers are those customers that tend to ask for the pricing of your goods or services prior to their attempting to find out specific details on how your product or service may be of value to them. Many customers of this caliber have some predetermined price point or value they have set for the product or service they are looking for.

An easy way to spot Talker behavior is that once sales information passes to the potential customer, additional customer action usually ceases and no sales occur.

A Talker has come into the sale negotiation with a predetermined market expectation (perhaps flawed) in which they have set the value of their patronage that you either meet or do not. Although changing a Talker's mind may be a very labor and time consuming effort of questionable return, they should always be treated with respect.

Do not be frustrated by this type of customer, even when they go so far as to ask you for a referral to another company providing the same

product or service your small business may provide (hint, directing customers to your competition takes a special kind of business strategy to be effective).

There is always the consideration of possible reward if successfully converting a Talker into a Doer.

A "Doer" actually buys your product or service, and quite often ends up acting as an unasked for referral source for your business.

Cherish them and make sure the customer understands you value their business! A reliable repeat customer is what you are aiming for.

To give this some real world context consider the following example.

Your author has been working in Taxation Law since 1959 and I have seen and have direct experience in a LOT of change since that time that include very dynamic markets that are almost unrecognizable at the time of this writing. I have had the time and inclination to study the market in my area very well, and with the reach of the internet have globally based clients as well.

I am a credible and credentialed professional with a long established business, proven reliable service (with credible references), and provide my services at very competitive rates for my market area.

I have tax and bookkeeping clients who ask me constantly for a "Good" Lawyer, Financial Planner, Real Estate Agent or advice on funding college education for kids, or re-investing funds.

Through my long career I have developed and maintained extensive business connections and have generally taken personal and professional delight in connecting people with resources they need. Everybody gets what they need and everyone is happy.

The complication comes from these customers being unclear on what exactly constitutes "good" to them.

Experience within my market has shown me this usually stems from a price point not within their expectation (i.e. too high for the value they have set) or they plainly unsure if they actually need a product or service, either due to confusion about the actual issue behind their inquiry or because they have trouble committing to a course of action.

For whatever reason, these customers never seem to follow up or make the referral contact based on information provided to them despite such actions being clearly in their best financial or personal interest.

These are my Talkers, but I treat them like my Doers.

The key difference from my Talkers versus Doer customers is that my Doer customer generally knows that they need a given product or service and continues to pursue information until they either succeed in obtaining it or understand they cannot afford it (for the moment). In other words they follow talk with action.

The Doer when it comes time actually makes the referral call, or buys the product or service even if they have determined that they can get it cheaper or for better value somewhere else.

But why would they do that? Why buy when you can get it cheaper elsewhere?

Demographics are excellent in aggregating a customer population's general characteristics and behavior patterns for a given sales market type, but people are not so narrowly defined that individually they may not conform to established demographic data.

Specific knowledge of your market demographics will assist you in targeting individual customers with advertisement information needed to try to turn the Talkers into Doers.

If you can target Talkers who can be transformed into Doers you increase your sales potential.

Since Doers often provide word of mouth advertising at no cost, this increases the potential for additional referrals that help to grow your business.

Talkers may end up having the opposite effect.

While you should always treat them with excellent customer service, understand that Talkers excel at talking – beware their providing unwarranted negative comments about the quality of your product or services that they have never likely experienced firsthand. You can run a quick internet search for many products that have talk forums that are filled with what amounts to negative advertisement.

It may be a fine line at times, particularly if your business requires direct sales interactions to customers (i.e. actually talking to them in person or on the phone), but you need to plan accordingly to politely disengage from Talkers who are not going to become Doers.

Time is money, and time is something you do not get back when it is wasted.

SBO Core Principle 9
Marsh's Theory of the Doubling Negative (-) Dollar.

Are your resources optimized to meet your endstate goals?

Small businesses expend a considerable amount of resources just staying in business, so it is crucial to your long term success in learning how to turn something that is having a negative impact on your business into a positive one whenever you can.

To be frank, you will not be able to avoid resource expenditures in running your business. Fortunately, there are some concepts we can apply to the small business world to help lessen that resource drain some. One way is embracing the concept that everything is a resource, even things like debt and expense.

While running your small business operations, you will deal with what are called 'Positive (+)' and 'Negative (-) resources.

In this example we will use the dollar as the identified resource and learn how to apply for your business the theory of the double negative dollar.

'Positive (+) $' Can be considered simple income generated, from any source.

'Negative (-) $' are any funds spent on any expenses.

Expenses may include (but are not limited to) payroll, taxes, supplies, product materials purchase or manufacture, vehicles, equipment, computers, business communications, electronics, product transport, and other like expenditures directly impacting your cash flow.

From these simplified definitions we can deduce that 'Negative (-) $' includes the dreaded Self-Employment (SE) Tax and ANY Negative (-) Loan Interest.

Now the Business Loan Interest is Tax Deductible...except you actually pay the Interest based at 100/cents-on-the-dollar($).

You are however Tax Deducting the same interest at your highest Internal Revenue Service (IRS) Nominal Marginal Individual or Corporate Tax Bracket at a set percentage rate (e.g. 15% to 28%, etc).

For EVERY 'Negative (-) $' you can eliminate from your Expense Spending Column (e.g. converting to a corporation entity that pays NO SE Taxes), that becomes ONE (1) 'Positive (+) $'.

So now, we have a case of changing 'Bad $' into 'Good $'.

So what you may wonder?

In the real world, that former 'Negative (-) $', now has the net practical effect of being worth two (2) 'Positive (+) $', funding that is much better spent being utilized in strengthening your new small business operation.

That is the true power and purpose for understanding the tagline:

'The Doubling Negative (-) Dollar ($)'

If you can capitalize on making expended resources work for you rather than against you, you are a step closer to making your endstate goals and achievable reality.

SBO Core Principle 10
The Unasked Question(s).

You have heard the saying "there is no stupid question?"

That is not the Unasked Question.

The Unasked Question (or Questions) is the sort of question whose answer could potentially make or break your small business.

So how do you know what those questions are?

Congratulations, you know quite a few of them already.

The very act of going through the SBO Core Principles exercise process should have sparked additional questions not specifically listed.

Take a few moments to freshly write down all the notes or questions that you do not have answers for yet.

For each Unanswered Question ask:

"Is this question relevant to my endstate goals?"

"Does potential answer to this question help or hinder or change my stated endstate goal?"

Your Unanswered Question list represents a good start to show you where you need to begin collecting information to fill gaps in your business plan that you may not have realized were there.

In the following chapters we will further expand on the SBO Core principles and explore how to use them to shape your business opportunities.

By setting your Draft SBO Endstate goals and using the SBO Core Principles, you now have taken the first steps toward developing yourself into a truly Dynamic Visionary, ready to make your business the financial success it deserves to be.

CHAPTER
-3-

"In the end, a vision without the ability
to execute it is probably an hallucination"

-Steve Case, co-founder AOL

To move a business product or service vision into an executable business plan, it is now time to move from theoretical to practical application of the SBO Core Principles discussed in the last chapter.

In running a 'For Profit' Small Business organization you will become familiar with those 'must do' or 'must have' business practices that you as an owner need to develop for your company foundation.

Let's start by defining the basic endstate of any small business as:

"The creation of a long term successful sustainable business, owned in whole or part by a single owner or form or partnership, that creates long term profit."

This generalized endstate is deliberately more vague than the endstate exercises you conducted from the last chapter, and is meant to provide an overarching framework for introduction to fundamental business startup concepts.

Your specific small business endstates will be refined in future chapter exercises and are designed to guide you through targeting achievable individual goals for your company.

Grab some fresh writing material again, and answer for yourself the following:

Is your small business endstate goal to run a long term business or to conduct a one off transaction?

This question is something you must know the answer to before proceeding on deciding what sort of business you want to set up.

As a Small Business Owner you must understand that having a marketable idea for a product or service is a single step in a long series to begin creating your small business.

A good idea alone however does not itself make a successful business.

This seems so obvious a conclusion as to not merit inclusion for discussion or instruction, but many potential business owners are caught unprepared for the realities of the time, planning, and resources it takes to remain in a long term operation intended to provide a comfortable living for themselves and their employees.

Creating a business is a legal commitment that may impact you, your family, friends, potential employees, and of course your customers.

Understanding that you are creating a business and not just a one time sale falls under the "Must Do" category of actions you must accomplish if you want to select the right kind of business you want to run.

Defining the Business

So what makes a 'For Profit' business?

A 'For Profit' business is fundamentally made up of two category components that work together to earn revenue that generates a profit.

40

Component One of an small business can be considered to include everything that constitutes the operational make-up of the business itself such as its people, logistics, product/service being provided, and any business dependencies.

This portion of your small business is the area that you as the owner have the greatest measure of direct control over. As a necessary consequence of the decisions you make to run your small business, Component One concerns contain some of the greatest opportunities to encounter business pitfalls that it is by default the focus of the majority of business development discussion that this book concentrates on.

Component Two of your small business is made up of your customers and Business Partners. More on them in a minute.

A 'Non-Profit Organization' or a 'Not-For-Profit' business on the other hand is a type of business usually founded for a specific purpose other than for generating profit. Note that these types of businesses can generate excess revenue (usually associated as profit in a 'For Profit' company), but that the excess revenue typically is used for achieving a specific goal rather than sharing or distributing profit to owners or partnerships as dividends.

Do not mistake a 'For Non-Profit' company as a company that does not earn revenue as you may be doing business with them in the future.

There are many legal requirements governing 'Non-Profit' organizations (which vary at the state, federal, and international level) and it is highly recommended the reader research specific details outside this publication if your goal is to pursue a 'Non-Profit' business. That said, most of the core business principles discussed and the business exercises provided do apply in the development of a 'Non-Profit' company as well.

Defining the Customer

So what is a customer?

A customer or patron is any person or entity that gives financial or other support to a person, organization, cause or activity.

A customer may be a one-time interaction or a regular and recurring source of incoming revenue for your business.

The Customer as described under Component Two is made up of any individual, purchasing groups, or other business entities that use your company's product or service.

Understanding who your customer is and how they fit within the market demographics of your business plan is falls directly under the "Must Have" knowledge category for your small business startup.

So why are customers important?

No customers equal no revenue and no profit.

No revenue means you are burning through your start-up resources without the long term means to sustain your business operations.

No profit means that your company is unable to re-invest in itself to grow or distribute earnings (which is sort of the whole point).

Take to heart that your customers are ultimately everything to your company. **EVERYTHING**.

Consider that even if you change the core product or service your company produces over time, you may be able to achieve a loyal customer base that purchases solely on brand loyalty if you have treated those customers with quality product and respect.

From the SBO Core Principles you came to understand that everything has potential value and cost. A customer is your chief resource to create revenue, a product or service is secondary.

Why?

If you have a product or service no one buys, you have little of value. A customer may not only purchase from you, they may lead others to become your customers.

Build value by treating customers well and they will lead more customers to you.

Every customer is different, but they may have similar needs or wants that you as a business owner will try to provide for.

In the last chapter SBO Core Principles we reviewed how customers can not only be categorized by market demographics, but how they also are also individuals.

Customers as a group usually display some behavior that is potentially predictable, while individuals may deviate wildly. Some of these are the Talker, and the more valued ones the Doers.

Due to the multitude of characteristics that make up a customer base, you will spend a significant amount of your company working hours and resources in trying to gain and retain their trust and patronage.

To build and retain your customer base you must embrace the attitude that you NEED to treat EVERY customer, client, and business partner as if they were the ONLY one you have.

Try writing down the following statement on your notes:

I will treat my customers as if they were the only one I have.

This is not a company endsate, but the beginning of a company mission or vision statement. This customer first approach is so vitally important that you should strongly consider making it your number one business directive for how you define and execute your Customer Service.

When you write out your formal business plan, ensure the cost of conducting proper Customer Service is factored in when making financial decision on what to spend on advertising, marketing, and employee training.

Everything in your business venture has a cost, including budgeting for activities necessary to make and retain your customers.

If your customers are a 'Must Have' then your efforts to attract and retain them are a 'Must Do'.

There is another special kind of customer we need to discuss, and that is the Business Partner.

The Business Partner relationship falls generally into two types:

A Business Partner is an individual or cooperate entity that might be a direct buyer of your goods or services (usually bought at a discount) who then sells your product at a retail store (for a retail markup).

This sort of retailer relationship is critical for a company that manufactures items and may form the bulk of your sales for your company.

A Business Partner may also be a supplier of materials needed in some capacity by your company to produce its products or services. If they are, then that Business Partner is a 'Must Have'.

This type of Business Partner may form a business dependency for your company, in such that the Business Partner provides something without which your business cannot function (such as a component or ingredient). Be very careful of creating business dependencies, particularly in product manufacturing.

In both cases, what and how that Business Partner acts have a direct impact on your own small business, particularly in the development of a reputation for your small business.

Treat a Business Partner poorly and expect to get burned.

While very simple business concepts, understanding that business resources and relationships form a series of 'Must Do' or 'Must Have' activities that your small business needs to address and upon which you will build its foundation.

For each business exercise in this book, keep these fundamentals in mind as you begin to answer for your new business.

At each stage of developing your endstate goal, ask "do the SBO Core Principles you need to apply form a Must Do' or 'Must Have' relationships?"

Complete these exercises to help generate more of the Unasked Questions needed to focus your business decisions on.

CHAPTER
-4-

"The only limits are, as always, those of vision."

- James Broughton, American Poet & Filmaker.

Pull out your SBO Core Principle exercise notes from Chapter-1 where you completed your draft endstate to determine your small business goal.

If you have not completed your draft yet with your own endstate goal, it is a good idea to go back to Chapter-1 now and have a go at it.

Once you are finished with your draft, have it on hand for this next round of exercises.

Do not worry if it is not perfect or complete, you will be doing this many times prior to actually starting your business.

When you wrote that endsate goal draft you gave yourself important clues as to what kind of business you want to have.

Now you will use your endsate goal notes and SBO Core Principles readings to start to begin refining what type of small business you are actually going to establish to form your Small Business Overhead Outline.

Over the following chapters you will ask yourself and answer in detail the following SBO Startup questions:

Question 1.   Why are you starting up your own business?

Question 2.   What type of business are you starting (or already have)?

Question 3.   What Type of business entity will your small business be classified as?

Question 4.   Capitalization. How will you fund your New Startup Small Business?

Question 5.   Location. Where will you conduct business from?

Question 6.   Record-Keeping. How are you going to keep records?

Question 7.   Depreciation. How can you defray overhead costs?

Question 8.   How are you going to conduct Payroll and Contract Labor?

Question 9.   Profit Margins. What is the Fair Market value of your product or service as a measure of Value Profit Margin?

Each question in turn is broken into its own chapter and includes a discussion on the topic question to give you context in developing an answer specific to your own small business venture.

CHAPTER
-5-

"Why climb the corporate ladder when
you can build an elevator in your own building?"

- Joshua E. Leyenhorst

Question 1.
WHY...are you starting up your own business?

Really ask yourself why you want your own business and write down the resulting answer.

Is it a Lifetime Goal, regardless of your own age?

Do you want to get rich, or just provide for a Qualified Retirement Plan to financially secure your Senior Moment years?

Do you just want to control your work hours?

Do you want to create something new?

Do you want financial independence to be your own boss?

Do you want to create jobs?

Do you want to create disruptive products to an industry?

Do you want to make a product or service more accessible to more people?

49

Do you want to improve a product or service you feel is deficient?

Do you want to connect with or remove yourself from direct contact with customers?

Do you want to learn something new?

Do you want to teach others?

Do you want to change the world, country, city, town, or neighborhood?

Depending on what your goal is, you may be setting up this business not just for yourself, but for your family or even to the ultimate benefit of a community or industry.

The list of possible motivations is nearly endless, but it is critical for you to understand WHY you are really doing this business venture before you commit the resources to it.

Covered briefly in the Chapter-1 Introduction, answering this question tests why you are starting your SBO and ultimately your commitment of effort to it.

Opening and operating your own small business is a serious commitment of time, money, resources, and acceptance of legal obligation that you personally are taking on as a small business owner.

By knowing the why, you firmly establish your foundation of your business vision that in turn aids you in determining your first endstate goal for your Business Plan.

With a specific endstate in mind you can walk-the-process-backward to the starting point you are at now to figure out how many resources (in time, employees, services, products, customers, capital, etc...) you need in order to accomplish your stated goal.

This is what is termed as a critical path moment.

Take some time to really think about why your motivation for starting this SBO since it will directly influence your answers to the foundation questions.

It may sound somewhat silly, but be absolutely sure that the business you are creating is the one you really want to run.

CHAPTER
-6-

"Success usually comes to those who
are too busy to be looking for it"

- Henry David Thoreau

Question 2.
What type of business are you starting
(or already have)?

In Chapter 3 you were introduced to the the differences between 'For Profit' and 'Not-For-Profit' business establishments. This is a foundational decision as to how your business may ultimately be governed by the laws, codes, and regulations your company may have to legally comply with.

How you decide to set up your small business is largely determined by the type of business category that you intend to compete in the market place with.

While each business category or type has similarities with the others, each also holds fundamental differences that directly impact how your business is actually run.

Before you make a decision on the business type that you as a SBO intend to run, lets review the most common types available.

Your business may fall into one or more of these business types:

The Expert Consultant

The Services Provider

The Manufacturer

The Wholesale Goods Seller

The Retail Goods Seller

The Franchise Operator

The Multi-market Owner

Review each business category now to determine which operation best fits the small business model you have chosen to develop.

The Expert Consultant.

An Expert Consultant SBO is a business that leverages expertise that a client has need of either in a singular or multidisciplinary manner.

Clients may range from the individual, industry business, or possibly a government organization operating in either for profit or a nonprofit manner. Given the type of expertise provided this may or may not entail individual risk or legal responsibilities/consequences for the company providing such expertise.

This type of business often produces an official final report or outcome of some kind as a product deliverable that the client will use to make a business or organizational decision.

Most of the time the final deliverable product or service has an agreed upon price negotiated prior to effort, but in some cases the company instead bills for time provided as well (many law firms use this format).

Government use of subject matter expert consultants such a designated geographic area of the environment is one example of this sort of business.

The Service Provider.

A Services Provider offers some specific service activity in return for profitable compensation.

There is some similarity to the Expert Consultant SBO, but usually resulting in a more tangible physical outcome. Lawn care service, tax preparation, legal firms, or beauty salons are examples of this sort of business.

The main risk here is that either the client is unhappy with the rendered service or the provider somehow damages the client's person or property. Traditionally the hardest part of this business is to price services low enough to make a profit and not to price oneself out of a market!

The Manufacturer.

This SBO operates by manufacturing and selling products either directly to the marketplace or through wholesale and retail companies.

Many small manufacturing companies, particularly those that produce limited product runs, hand made, or unique items not suitable to large scale production, fall into this business type. Examples include SBOs that sell custom made trinkets or fresh produce at a local farmer's market.

Large scale manufacturers cover a significant portion of available goods that tend to be created in high volumes with set variations. Retail clothing, automobiles, computers, and cheap plastic novelties are typical of large scale manufacturing.

The large manufacturer may represent a significant challenge to your business model if you are competing against another company in the same product category. Due to the relative low cost per item, each large company must sell at a high volume to remain profitable, which if there are two or more manufacturers of a certain type may flood a market.

Large scale manufacturers often provide a community with significant employment and have deep legal pockets to defend against newcomers to their field.

Risks for any manufacturer include company liability for the quality of goods and health impacts to the users. Additionally, there may be research and development costs required to certify a product type for sale that may be hard earn a return on investment even over a long sales period.

When a manufacturer sells directly to a buyer, customer service often directly impacts actual sales, particularly in a crowded market scenario where perception of a product or business quality and reputation has a disproportionate impact on the customer's willingness to buy at a given price point.

The Wholesale Goods Seller.

An SBO that operates by Selling Wholesale Goods is one that usually deals in the buying and selling of materials or products used by other companies in a retail setting.

This type of business covers the sale of large scale quantity items such as tee shirts, retail clothing, the harvesting and sale of raw goods or materials such as unfinished wood or produce, to even books like this for sale.

Wholesale items are usually sold to retailers at a sometimes shockingly (to the new SBO) low price. Publishers for example typically sell books at over a 60 percent markdown from expected retail price to the book

stores to ensure that their published product is carried and edges out shelf space to their higher cost competitor volumes. The remaining 40 percent would have to cover the cost of shipping, manufacture, administrative overhead, taxes, any expected profit, oh and the cost of paying the author which was minimal.

Modern manufacturing processes have not only generally increased the volume of production levels possible, but also have significantly minimized the manufacturing time. This combination acts as a business multiplier to make money as a consequence of the volume of operations for a given market.

But how does that work?

Consider that an individual wholesale good item may sell for mere pennies, but when sold in bulk adds up to a profitable good when sold in the thousands to millions of units range.

Remember seeing those cheap toy plastic rings or other toys kids get from gumball machines or dollar store vendors?

The steel die mold used for plastic mold injection to produce a simple plastic ring tends to run in the hundreds of thousands of dollars for tooled machinery despite the end product plastic result itself being exceptionally cheap. Multiply the sales of such cheaply produced goods by millions of times and the steel die mold that has a reuse life measured in years may pay for itself over a relatively short period Return On Investment (ROI).

This sort of business also tends to be very heavy with logistics overhead requirements, particularly in warehousing and transportation expense (including likely dealing with international customs regulations). Risk here includes the mentioned logistics overhead costs and the potential with getting stuck with significant bulk product that may suddenly stop selling.

Record keeping and facilitating sales are make or break characteristics of this type of SBO.

The Retail Goods Seller.

Of course a very common SBO is the activity of Selling Retail Goods.

These are businesses that buy wholesale finished goods and sell them at a retail markup they believe their buyers will purchase at. This is primarily why you see different prices at different stores for the same item. Many online companies are quite successful despite a buyer finding multiple price points for the same item since the business itself is largely about instilling trust in the company and connecting people with items they want at an affordable price.

Pricing correctly is a make or break point for these type of businesses, and a greater overhead expenditure is likely to be spent on developing a brand identity despite the company not actually manufacturing the item being sold.

While product quality is a significant factor, perception of value for a product brand generally runs higher (recall earlier discussion on customer perception). This is why some fashion retail stores sell a dress for hundreds of dollars one season, and yet it drop it by 75% or more the next. This might be due to the changing of the season so there is a need to get rid of dead stock or a fashion trend simply wearing itself out. This business behavior is particularly evident in companies that specialize in products with a built in obsolescence factor such as some computer software that require subscription models.

Examples of this type of SBO are the small general store, clothing retailer, special item seller, or even online auctions.

Key characteristics for this SBO include location (physical and on the internet) and advertising.

Customer Service for this type of business is critical; ignore it at your own peril.

The Franchise Owner.

The Franchise Owner SBO is a special case.

This is where you buy into an existing franchise which provides you with almost everything you need to run that franchise to include a business plan and access to established material, distribution networks, and advertising resources under a defined brand name. Many of the most popular fast food restaurants fall into this category. The main risk is usually the very high cost of buying a franchise versus the time it takes to earn a return on investment.

The buy-in cost risk may be mitigated somewhat by having access to the franchise parent corporation resources, but it also entails acceptance of risk for when that parent corporation does something not in the best interest of your individual franchise ownership.

Loss of some business control due to actions of the parent corporation can be a big factor in an individual franchise location failing, such as the franchise owner possibly not the having final say on a given storefront location due to the parent franchise company trying to constrain a competitor by flooding a market area with similar products or services. If you have ever wondered why so many fast food chains or big box store are right across the street from each other this is a prime reason despite a known limited customer base.

The Multi-market Owner.

Of the many possible categories, many SBOs tend to restrict themselves when starting out to just a single category. Enter the Muli-Market Owner, that may be a service provider, consultant, and whole seller, each business type being either related or individually different yet run under a corporate core business.

Often to grow a business, the SBO may delve into multiple business types over time as a means to diversify.

Settling on the sale of a single product, even with multiple models or configurations available at the highest quality can be a very risky venture. Some products naturally have a limited lifespan, whether due to advancing technology, material availability, or fashion trends

Keep in mind that business growth may be essential to the long term business plan of your SBO, but reckless growth that does not take into consideration the following questions is begging for trouble.

How many different products can you afford to sell?

Hoe many of each product type should you keep in stock?

Is there an overhead cost such as a licensing fee to maintain and is it sustainable over the expected lifetime of the product?

Remember, everything has an overhead cost of some type, so when you carry multiple lines those costs tend to increase. On the other hand, carrying multiple product lines usually ensures that the SBO helps to insulate itself from their only product suddenly no longer selling and endangering company revenue intake outright.

This is the "don't put all your eggs in one basket approach" which seems sensible except that "too many eggs will break the basket".

Failing to balance risk in this sort of venture can drain critical resources from the other parts. Combined with the need to maintain complex logistics and regulatory compliance, the Multi-Market SBO can make central management exceptionally time consuming and challenging.

Most of the largest retail goods companies fall into this category, offering items that range from infant toys to household appliances. These are the super big-box stores that range from massive brick and mortar outlets to warehouse shipping from on online portal.

What company type is right for my Small Business model?

By taking the time to study what sort of company you are creating, you help to narrow your risks by understanding who your competition is, what your cost of doing business may entail, and what sort of legal obligations you may be incurring.

You should match your draft endstate goal with your product or service idea to see how it best matches with the type of business will work best for you.

It is important to note that you you must study your local, state, and federal laws (or applicable country laws if doing business outside your own) to be sure you have a clear understanding of rules, regulations, codes and laws that may apply to your business type.

DO NOT ASSUME

Business can be a very odd place with all sorts of subtle influences since it is built on laws, codes, and even customs that have evolved over time. Do not assume you understand them all or the interaction between them until you have taken the time to study them in depth. In that study you may find that something you thought was trivial becomes instead a critical aspect to your business success.

Success ultimately means not only knowing the field you are striving to do business in, but how your company can compete in that field.

CHAPTER
-7-

"Stop Chasing the money and start chasing the passion."

- Tony Hsieh

Question 3.
What Type of business entity
will your SBO be classified as?

Once you have determined what type of business you are going to run, you will need to understand how that business is classified under the laws that govern it.

There are several types of For-Profit Business Entity classifications to choose from in the United States (other countries have their equivalents).

Just like each business type, each business classification structure has their place and uses for you to consider when initially establishing your company.

It is possible to start a business under one classification and later switch it to another. If you think you will change business classifications at some future time, be aware that converting your SBO to a different type of business type or classification may require legal assistance to accomplish. As always, learn the specific details involved and plan ahead to make it easier for any later changes.

The most common legally recognized classification of business entities for establishing the Small Business Ownership include:

The Sole Owner/Sole Proprietor with or without a Limited Liability Company (LLC) status.

The Partnership/LLC Partnership

The C-Type Corporation

The S-Type Corporation

Review each business category in depth prior to selecting which is right for your small business development.

The Sole Owner/Sole Proprietor with or without a Limited Liability Company (LLC) status.

Starting with one of the most common and simplest SBOs to establish, the Sole Owner/Sole Proprietor with or without a Limited Liability Company (LLC) is a type of business status that is not considered a separate legal entity, rather it simply refers to an individual who owns the SBO and is responsible for its debts.

A sole proprietorship may operate under the name of its owner, or under a fictitious trade name such as "Ed's Barbershop" or something flavorful as "The Juice Pit" (which may have nothing to do with juice).

To establish a Sole Owner/Sole Proprietor with or without a Limited Liability Company (LLC) status as a business entity, register the Certificate with your local County Clerk as a non-LLC DBA (Doing-Business-As) your name or trade name.

If an LLC is desired (which is VERY highly recommended for its $40 million dollar worth of Liability Coverage in most US States), apply to your State Secretary of State (SOS), or its local State equivalent.

The usual one-time cost is a business expense deductible.

Fees will vary from State-to-State, but are not unreasonable (e.g. $300.00 flat fee in Texas).

Next if you are in the United States (for other countries see local government laws as applies for details) you will need to go to the Internal Revenue Service at www.irs.gov to get a free IRS Employer Identification Number (EIN). Note that both an Entity Document and the SBO EIN are usually needed to open-up a business checking account with your local bank or credit union.

During United States tax season, you will file IRS Schedule-C (Sole Owner) or Schedule-F (Farm or Ranch), both of which will you will pay an extra 15.30% (as of this publication, see IRS for current rates) Self-Employment (SE) Taxes when filing your Individual Form 1040, as well as Income Taxes on your Basic Net Profits. If you are operating your business from your home, remember that Home Office deductions apply to the Schedule-C ONLY. If you are an Owner of Rental Income Property, you file IRS Schedule-E and no SE Taxes apply.

The Partnership/LLC Partnership.

The Partnership/LLC Partnership is established by applying to the State Secretary of State (SOS) or equivalent. This sort of business entity is made up of 2 or more Individuals or organizations to form a formal US Domestic Partnership. As with a Sole Owner/Sole Proprietor with or without a Limited Liability Company (LLC) status company, a Partnership/LLC Partnership will also require its own IRS Employer Identification Number (EIN).

For Tax reporting, each Partner tracks Earned Income Taxed on his or her own Form 1040, Page 2, Schedule E, PLUS (+) the 15.30% Self-Employment (SE) Taxes. Each Partner further receives a Form K-1, to lateral the dollar amount to their own Form 1040.

A major difference between the Sole Owner/Sole Proprietor with or without a Limited Liability Company (LLC) status company and a Partnership is that each partner that forms the formal US Domestic Partnership has a percent share in the total Partnership.

This means sharing ownership and unlimited legal liability responsibility, including debts and liabilities of each partner.

In a Partnership, each Partner may be held liable for the negligence of other partners. In a LLC Partnership, the company has a separate legal existence separate from its owners, providing some legal protection, principally in the form of protecting a Partner's personal assets.

In a LLC Partnership, a Partner's personal assets may not be used to cover the LLC Partnership business debts, and liability for those business debts does not extend beyond the amount invested in the percent shared in the LLC Partnership.

The C-Type Corporation.

The C-Type Corporation under United Stets federal income tax law is any corporation (including almost all for-profit companies) that is taxed separately from its owners.

To establish a C-Type Corporation, Apply to the State Secretary of State (SOS) or equivalent (you should start to see a pattern forming here for each business type). A C-Type Corporation may have any number of shareholders (both foreign and domestic) with Preferred Stock Shares and/or Common Stock shares.

The C-Type Corporation, like other businesses entities, requires an Employer Identification Number (EIN).

Examples of this type of corporation include: Microsoft, Apple, and General Electric.

The C-Type Corporation is taxed as a separate business entity from its shareholders and files IRS Form 1120. As a United States corporation the company pays its own Federal & State Income Taxes. Note that State Tax rates may vary. The Federal tax rate is a Flat 21% (as of this publication) on the first $50,000.00 Net Earnings (Profits). C-Type Corporations do not pay the extra 15.30% Self Employment Tax paid by Solo Schedules C or US Domestic Partnerships.

Always go to the IRS website or tax publications for the most up to date tax rates.

The C-Type Corporation can either pay that amount (+ under-tax-payment interest owed) when e-filing your Form 1120 by providing the company Business Checking Account Number and 9-digit Bank Routing Number or payment may be made through the Electronic Federal Tax Payment System (EFTPS). Go to www.irs.eftps.gov to set up this type of account. Exempt from SE taxes on Net Earnings. Also, needs an Employer Identification Number (EIN).

C-Type Corporations are required to issue financial statements in the United States. Financial statements are presented on any comprehensive basis including the income tax basis. If the C-Type Corporation is publicly traded, then it also falls under the Sarbanes-Oxley Act of 2002 under Public Law 107-204 and must appoint auditors as part of its taxation process.

The S-Type Corporation.

The S-Type Corporation under United States federal income tax law is a closely held corporation, in many cases formed under a limited liability or partnership, that makes a valid election to be taxed under sub-chapter 'S' of Chapter 1 of the Internal Revenue Code.

The S-Type Corporation directly pays NO Federal taxes, instead the corporation's income or losses are divided through its shareholders.

Shareholders of an S-Type Corporation report their share of the company income or loss on their own individual tax returns rather than from the company as an independent business entity.

S-Type Corporations may be small qualifying SBO that have grown into very successful corporations and include such examples as Walmart, Toys R' Us, and Mars, Incorporated.

ONLY the IRS grants S-Type Corporation status.

An S-Type Corporation is converted through submission and acceptance of the IRS Form 2553 to convert a Limited Liability Company (LLC), Partnership, LLC Partnership, or a Form 1120 C-Type Corporation. The S-Type Corporation Employer Identification Number (EIN) is usually taken from the type of business entity being converted.

The S-Type Corporation has several restrictions over other business entity types. The S-Type Corporation is defined as a small business corporation under section 1362(a) of the Internal Revenue Code and so to be eligible for conversion an S-Type Corporation must be a domestic corporation (LLC or a Partnership) with no more than 100 shareholders (spouses and estates are treated as a single shareholder), not have a shareholder who is not an individual (there are exceptions such as estates and trusts), have more than one class of stock (all outstanding sock confers identical rights to distribution and liquidation proceeds), and may not have as a shareholder a nonresident alien.

For tax reporting, S-Type Corporation shareholders are allocated Net Earnings according to their company percent shares through the Form K-1 which is lateraled to Form 1040, Page 2, Schedule E. Of considerable note is that an S-Corporation shareholder pays no Self-Employment (SE) Taxes. Under the Tax Cuts & Jobs Act of 2017, this type of corporation and Domestic Partnerships receive a favored-status deduction of their bottom-line Net Income (Profits) on their Form 1220s US Corporation Tax Return.

Understand the complex legal obligations and plan accordingly.

CHAPTER
-8-

"Do not let the fear of loosing be greater than
the excitement of winning"

- Robert Kiyosaki

Question 4.
Capitalization. How will you fund your
New Startup Small Business?

Wanting to start a business and having a good idea is one thing, but do you have the resources too actually do it? That old cliche that states it takes money to make money is entirely all to true.

Your SBO startup going to need money to get started, but how much do you really need?

Where do you get funding if you do not have enough?

What are some of the risks involved with gaining startup capital?

Is your funding source personal Savings, Individual or Company Investors, Family Gifts, existing Qualified or Unqualified Retirement funds, Promissory Note, or some other Signature or Financial House Loans needed to secure a business loan to include loans from the Small Business administration (SBA)?

When you begin an SBO, adequate capitalization dollars are needed for a host of Startup expenses and to cover the first few years of business operations.

To know what sort of starting funding you will need, you will need to do a some form of Business Financial Plan to accurately predict and project ALL of your known or expected income to cover your typical business expenses such as payroll and payroll Federal & State Taxes.

For this exercise, add to your your pencil and paper a calculator as well. Given how complex accounting for these costs can be, it may now be a good time to use (and learn) a spreadsheet or accounting program so you can easily adjust figures when doing your analysis.

Start by recording your projected funding expenses and income over a 12-month period and a 36-month period.

In this example, try working through the concept that you are going to need to lease space in a business zone for your small business operations. Do not worry if this may not fit your current plans, this exercise is meant to have you run through some of the thought processes you need to mentally gear yourself into thinking about.

For this exercise you are using a Storefront or Commercial Office rental for your SBO, with the typical scenario that you expect to sign an initial Lease contract for at least three years or 36 months with a Storefront Liability Insurance Policy.

Under most US State Laws (and many other countries), you OWE 36 months of Rent or Lease payments in addition to deposits, possibly utilities, maintenance fees, and possible space build-out costs. Already you are now counting on needing this 36-month amount in income to account for this overhead requirement.

So what else?

You should consider in your business plan the scenario that you might have to break the terms of your rental or leasing contract.

To factor in this possibility, usually the first and last month are 100% funding requirements. This assumes of course that you can break the lease contract without owing the entire signed lease contract amount (which may require lawyer services with associated costs) during which other penalties and fees may also apply.

In other words READ and UNDERSTAND your lease completely before you sign, and ASK, ASK, ASK for clarification from the leasing company or your property agent/lawyer if there is anything you do not understand. This sort of contract is very tedious to read in depth, but you need to ensure that you understand each legal clause, especially the ones that you expect never to happen such as determining who is financially responsible for the property damage in case of a fire?

The key point from this example is that you start incurring costs almost immediately BEFORE you have actually sold anything. That money has to come from somewhere.

For your business plan, you need to consider the cost drivers for a physical location. A storefront or office finishing-out, unless covered by the Landlord or Property Manager within your lease agreement, are often on YOUR 'dime'. Consider that operational expenses are more than employees and normally include monthly utilities, such as gas, electric, water, landline office or mobile telephones, as well as cable/satellite television connections, and internet connectivity.

There may be newspaper and magazine subscriptions in many business environments where your Clients, Patients, or Customers are seated in a tastefully, well-equipped Waiting Room or Lounge Area complete with free incentive amenities such as wireless internet access or a water cooler.

Again much to take into account beyond just the signature on a lease.

71

Additional startup costs include the requirement to properly equip your storefront, office, manufacturing area, or warehouse (this also applies to home businesses). These include both durable items (things you will use repeatedly) and expendable items. Examples of durable items include furniture and furnishings, computers, phones, work stations, office equipment for printing, copying, faxing & scanning, and manufacturing.

Examples of expendable items (things used up during business activities as single use items) include office business supplies (e.g. ink/toner and copy paper), janitorial supplies (toilet paper, paper towels; disinfectant; mops/brooms, etc.), and most raw materials used in the manufacture of goods.

So what does all this tell you?

Due to the financial requirements inherent in a physical location, it is not recommended for a new SBO to have a lease extend beyond three years and it is highly recommended to secure initial funding to cover the time period of the lease as part of your base business planning.

If you are not going to lease (or own) a property, where else might you consider operating your company? If your services or sales lend themselves to your own Home Office, you STILL need to equip it, but costs can be defrayed by exercising "The Law of Intent."

With the Law of Intent, you take personally owned items (i.e. furniture/ furnishings, computers, electronics, etc...) and CHANGE their Original Intent, by consciously converting them to Home Office Business Use.

One way is to convert your 'priciest' items, so you fully depreciate them as part of Your Home Owner Deductions (if your Business is organized as a Solo or Solo LLC IRS Schedule C.)

Capitalization dollars will also be needed for Marketing and Advertising your business to draw and keep customers to your SBO.

Such cost outlays may include an internet web site, advertising through web ads on established web sites, newspaper and circular ads, direct phone contact (although this has lost favor recently) if selling to individuals, catalog production, mailing fliers, and possibly even television commercials.

Note that e-mail ads are not suggested due to the high number of SPAM e-mails and phishing attempts that have rendered potential customers very wary of a positive response from unsolicited e-mail contact.

For each level of your business plan, think about what else you might need funding for in the first 36 months.

You will need access to a Cash Reserve for any unexpected events.

Examples include income receipt lower than projected for a given period or product, casualty or liability insurance deductibles, repairs and maintenance that are NOT the responsibility of the Landlord or Commercial Property Manager, or commercial common area or strip center Leasing Fees.

Figure out not only what you need to spend funds on, but what you might be able to do without.

What is a need for the business and what is a want?

This is where you can also try to reduce unexpected expenses by 'looking-over-the-horizon,' and by anticipating the most likely "Worse Case Scenarios" you might encounter dollar-wise.

Once you have that worst case number, multiply that two-fold to give you an estimate on how much capital reserve you are likely to need at any given time during the first 36 months.

Assume-the-Worse, but Plan for-the-Best.

NEVER Hope for a productive resolution to a crisis, always take decisive action when you need to.

All the above common sense examples apply BEFORE your money needs to go to the purchase of basic product source items (if manufacturing), or to Resell COGS (Cost-of-Goods-Sold Product).

A very common source of small business failing comes from owners who do not adequately plan for overhead costs not directly related to their product or service creation.

Another way to fail is to fail to anticipate the cost of success.

If you are engaged in manufacturing are you logistically prepared to fill orders of dozens or even hundreds of units?

Your Business and Marketing Plans need to take projected and unexpected success into account, of at least 25% to 50% over-sales capacity of your goods or service. This initial funding projection may result in your company needing more capital funding than you have available and present you with the unexpected problem of being in too high a demand that you are unable to deliver.

If you cannot deliver there will be a price to pay.

See Chapter 15 on the importance of managing your company reputation.

Ultimately, creating your detailed business plan is essential to success. Take the time to try to conceive of as many possible outlays of funding you may need to cover for the first 36 months.

Once you are secure in that, start to plan for the next 36 months. This is a cycle that will end only when you are ready to either sell your business or shutter it for good.

Your business is a living breathing entity, you must tend to it for it to grow and bloom into the success you know it can be.

CHAPTER
-9-

"Something like 80 percent of business decisions have a location element. In fact, it's probably higher than that."

- Jack Dangermond

Question 5.
Location. Where will you conduct business from?

The importance of where your small business is located has been discussed quite a bit already in the preceding chapters, particularly regarding your market analysis.

The key takeaway is that the place you determine for your business location will shape much of your business dealings and much of your initial business plan assessment. It also sets a timer, if your business grows quickly you may outgrow your available space faster than you expect.

Consider for a moment that the business location itself is a tool that will help or hinder certain aspects of your ability to sell your product or service.

Where your business is located determines availability of customer foot traffic, how much it costs to transport goods to or from its location, to what kind of work you can even do at that location.

At this point in the exercises, you have determined what your business type is and what product or service it is that you intend to provide for sale.

A business location typically is considered the location from which a point of sale is made to a customer, however it may be a place that includes administration, warehousing, or manufacturing requirements.

First, lets take a look at some examples of how deciding where your business location is placed has impacts on the

Compare how location influences the following sample business types:

If you are a manufacturer, the place where you conduct your business may need to include space for cutting and assembly equipment, enough utilities to power that equipment, testing areas, painting areas, packaging areas, a loading dock, and warehousing space in addition to administrative space for records, bathrooms, break areas, waiting areas, possibly display or research space. Then there is parking to consider for yourself, company transportation, employees.

Is this manufacturing space the show area for clients to view products?

How far is it to ship products from your location to reach the customer?

How close is your manufacturing facility to shipping services (land, sea, or air)?

What is the cost of shipping from this location?

Is the area where the manufacturing occurs zoned properly for this type of work (particularly environmental and sound considerations)?
How much product can be manufactured at this location and how much stock can be held before manufacturing must stop?

What about environmental concerns? How are you getting rid of manufacturing waste? Is it toxic?

Is this location rated for this sort of manufacturing waste, and can you afford the risk of environmental cleanup penalties and fees?

How close is your manufacturing facility to material supply locations?

If you are running this manufacturing business out of your home, you may have an immediate need to relocate if you become quickly successful (assuming you can even legally run this business from a residential area).

Can you afford the down time in manufacturing if you have to move locations? For how long?

If you are a wholesaler, you are likely receiving product and shipping that product back out. Where you locate your warehouse space impacts your transportation, holding capacity, and shipping costs in both directions if you take returns on products.

Products that do not sell or are broken take up space and reduce your capacity to sell products that earn you revenue. Remember, even if you are not successful at selling anything you are still paying for the location overhead. In the IRS World, any unsold COGS Inventory is considered as SOLD and counts as Taxable Income. Remove all damaged or obsolete unsold product from your Year-End-Inventory to save on income tax or Self Employment Tax (if applicable).

The retail business owner may operate out of a storefront or a stand alone structure, If a standalone structure, all of the above applies plus the need to drive foot traffic to your location.

Each type of storefront has its advantages and disadvantages.

A shopping mall or strip outlet may contain many different types of businesses that attract a wide variety of customer types. Ensuring that you place your business within a location that creates synergy with your business is crucial.

Placing your business in strip mall that has nothing in common with your business may mean that you are not only not reaching your target demographics for sales, but those same other customer types are taking up parking that keeps your customers from reaching you!

If your business location is in a bad part of town (even just the perception of such) it will lower your customer traffic and therefore your odds of making a sale. This is the type of location that the Talkers Customer mentioned previously will generally use as a basis to call your product quality into question, by equating it poor quality with a seedy looking storefront.

If you are running a service of some type, then the type of service will dictate your space requirements and your location may directly impact your ability to make sales.

A service oriented business like a tax consultant has primarily administrative space consideration, waiting area requirements, and paper file storage.

A service oriented business such as a maid's for hire may need parking space for company vehicles and storage space for stocking cleaning products.

For most types of business locations you need to be able to answer the following:

Can I afford the rent, utilities, building ownership or strip mall fees?

What is the parking situation for your employees (if any), yourself, and most importantly your customers or clients?

Does locale traffic patterns and vehicle flow keep customers from me or hinder me from providing my goods or services to my customers in any way?

Is the proposed business location easy for customers to reach, enter, and exit?

Does this location have some unique feature that will make a BIG difference in the ultimate success or failure of your chosen enterprise?

Can your intended buyers find your business?

The second part of the equation for determining your location is understanding how that location interacts with not only your customers, but where your business competition may be.

If a commercial Storefront or office, you MUST know where your competition is within a 5-10 miles Radius from your chosen business location.

Competition is just that, their job is to make money, and if your business is a success at that location then it shows them there are customers for them to sell to.

The reverse is true as well if you are establishing a new business in an area with existing businesses. Generally it is much more difficult to establish a new business that offers the same products or services as your competitors. Common ways to mitigate competition include appealing to a customer perceived dissatisfaction on available products or services offered by your business competition, having some disruptive technology or process that lets you vastly undercut your competition's prices, or by coming in with the support of a large franchise brand that customers are already familiar with.

But how do you gain information about a prospective business location that is outside your home?

There is significant demographics information you can pull from your State, County, and City (there are also country briefs for international business interests) that can aid you in your business location selection.

It is also highly advisable that you drive and walk the site under consideration during the hours of business that you intend to operate. Make note of activities in the ares during the hours of business, check on customer traffic, and determine if you have or will have a competitor in the same business field at or near that location.

All these are logistical considerations when running your business.

Logistics is the detailed coordination of complex operations, involving many people, facilities, or supplies.

The location of your business will drive many of the critical factors in your business logistics flow.

There is an old military saying that says,

"Forget Logistics, and you lose."

If you forget about how your business location impacts the many intersections of your business logistics, your business will likely fail.

Do not forget logistics.

CHAPTER
-10-

"Documents create a paper reality we call proof"

- John Conyers

Question 6.
Record-Keeping. How are you going to keep records?

Record-Keeping.

This term invokes unnecessary dread it seems for many starting business owners.

Some reasons often cited?

Record-keeping is not generally considered the fun part of business.

Record-keeping may be considered boring or tedious.

Record-keeping may be viewed as taking time away from conducting the part of the business that generates revenue.

Record-keeping may be overwhelming to someone where detail is not their strongest skillset.

Record-keeping is a critical aspect of business logistics.

Let's be clear:

Any business owner who ignores the aspect of record-keeping for their business does so at their own peril.

If you do not keep good records your business WILL most likely fail.

And if you really do not keep good records?

If you are lucky you may just pay a hefty fine, but you also might go to jail.

Why?

Because most countries, states, cities, and counties have laws and regulatory codes that require you to keep accurate and complete records. Failure to do so could range from a warning, to a fine, to time in prison.

Your record-keeping is proof your company did something, and lack of it generally assumes your company did not do something plain and simple.

Need to prove that your product could not have poisoned someone with toxic materials?

What do you think the courts are going to look for when you get sued?

So what can good record-keeping do for you?

Good record-keeping helps maintain a clear audit trail that:

Tracks information that allows you to make good business decisions such as how much product to sell, for how much, or when to switch to a new product or hire more employees.

Clean records help you find information quickly and accurately which is critical when dealing with customer service issues.

Detailed records help you accurately deal with your suppliers.

It helps you to prepare documentation and prove to a bank or private lender investors your company is worthy of a loan or investment.

Records are needed to meet regulatory requirements and defend against lawsuits.

But the principle reason besides complying with the law to keep accurate records, is ensuring all your tax information is correct.

Keeping your product stock or service records accurate will ensure you know when, where, and by whom your company is receiving revenue from to capitalize sales or where your company may be bleeding money.

You may use either computer or manual methods when keeping records, or in the case of larger business, be required by law to keep both for an extended period of time. Ensure that you maintain and keep any specific record types required by codes or regulations up to date and accessible by the appropriate company leadership.

These records compile information on your company.

Information provides you the power to ACT.

There are many available computerized business tools available to assist you in processing and categorizing your record information. These range from spreadsheets to various forms of information databases.

Of increasing utility now emerging are computer programs known as business intelligence tools (go ahead and look some up on the internet now) that allow you to create what is called a data cube to connect related data together.

This sort of software allows you to easily sort and parse the information into usable chunks to help you ask and answer specific questions that could aid in your company decision making process.

Assuming your business is fully within the boundaries of regulatory and legal compliance, the one thing your company will do regardless of its business type is pay taxes.

All businesses need to organize Income and Expenses by category.

Whomever is designated as the company bookkeeper should familiarize themselves with the specific Internal Revenue Service (IRS) forms that pertain to the business. Note that the bookkeeper is not the one ultimately responsible for anything incorrect, responsibility for the company ALWAYS includes the owners and/or partnership.

Refer to the IRS government website for the forms for:

Solo/Solo LLC Schedule C

Rental Owner Schedule E

Farm/Ranch Schedule F

Form 1065 (US Partnership)

Forms 1120/1120S (US Corporations)

Good record keeping can be accomplished by either physical records or through computerized records, or a combination of both.

The SBO has several options to consider for their bookkeeping/accounting startup:

The Computer Accounting Program.

This is a downloaded Computer Program or Online Accounting Service that utilizes a computer-based spreadsheet, or accounting database where business transactions can be tracked. Most programs allow you to create your own 'Income' and 'Expenses' categories to track your specific requirements based on the business IRS Form or schedule being filed.

Always be sure to post your business entries timely and be sure that the computer program provides monthly, quarterly, and annual year-end Grand Totals.

The Manual accounting method.

This is the original methods most people are familiar with which includes the usage of ledgers backed up with all types of receipts.

This system is time intensive, but no less effective than a computer based system when performed correctly and diligently.

Small business owners have used everything from envelopes, shoe-boxes, to filing cabinets to categorize expenses, keep receipts, and maintain income and bank Statement documents.

Some businesses (particularly medical companies) are required to keep physical records for specified periods of time regardless of their use of computer records that may actually be the source of the physical record copies themselves. If your company must keep physical records, be sure to account for both the current and future space that will be required to house those records at your business location.

Like its computerized counterpart, maintain expenses segregated by category (see your appropriate IRS form or schedule).

It is highly recommended that the SBO keep running totals frequently (at a minimum quarterly), so that compiling the records is not an overwhelming task at Tax Filing time in transferring those totals to the correct IRS Entity Form or Schedule.

Whichever method you utilize be sure to maintain the records for the required number of years as it pertains to your business type.

Manual records should be kept in a climate controlled environment that is dry, but within a fire control area. Critical records that cannot be duplicated or replaced easily should be kept within a fire proof safe.

Regardless of the record-keeping method, be sure to have a thorough backup process for your records in case of fire or some other scenario that may damage or destroy the originals.

Remember, your records are your proof you did things right.

ALWAYS have backups for your most important financial records.

CHAPTER
-11-

"Today people who hold cash equivalents feel comfortable. They shouldn't. They have opted for a terrible long-term asset, one that pays virtually nothing and is certain to depreciate in value"

- Warren Buffett

Question 7.
Depreciation. How can you defray overhead costs?

There are many overhead costs your company will have to absorb over time.

While the US Internal Revenue Service (IRS) is not well known for its generosity, the recognition of the need to stimulate business through incentives of various kinds for the good of the economy and the development of new goods and services has led to the practice of allowing business deductions during tax collection.

Depreciation is a form of tax deduction that enables a business owner to offset income due to the continual decline in the value of owned property.

As per the US Code:

"He / She who OWNS, Depreciates."

An SBO may take an annual income tax deduction on property listed as an expense on an income statement. This allows an owner to reduce the value of an asset over a duration of time due to age or material decay from use.

Examples of assets that typically qualify for depreciation are tangible buildings, equipment, machinery, office furniture, work vehicles or intangible property such as patents or copyrights. These include any Single Line Item either bought, 'found,' gifted, or bartered (traded-for).

Per the IRS, Property you may not depreciate includes actual land (not buildings or improvement), company product inventory (which is meant for sale), or leased property (it is not considered "Owned" by the business).

Depreciation is considered non-cash expense, as such it is important to understand that it does not affect your small business cash flow.

So how does depreciation work?

For starters you must be the rightful owner of the property asset and that asset must have a useful life of at least one year. Such items placed on a Depreciation schedule MUST cost or have a Fair Market Value of greater than $100.00 to include the State Sales Taxes.

Assets have a purchase value and a Salvage Value. A Salvage Value is the amount you could sell the asset for during a period of its useful life.

The IRS requires that your business starts to depreciate the qualifying asset once in use, and to stop depreciating the value when you have fully recovered the cost of the asset.

Remember that you cannot depreciate the asset for more than the cost of the asset, not what it may be worth.

Straight-Line Method Depreciation.

Assets have longevity lives of 3, 5, 7, 10, 15, etc... years.

To 100% depreciate assets under the Straight-Line Method of depreciation they must be retained in business use for that long.

Common Depreciation Years Examples:

Software	3-years
Light Trucks/Cars	5-years
Furniture	7-years
Computers/Electronics/Telephones	7-years
Land Improvements	15-years
Residential Income Real Estate	27.5-years
Commercial Real Estate	39-years

This type of depreciation write off is calculated as an equal annual amount each year until the qualifying asset is fully depreciated.

To do this first calculate:

Asset Cost - Asset Salvage Value = Depreciation Cost

Then calculate:

Depreciation Cost / Useful Life in Years =

Annual Depreciation Expense

Example:

If a a piece of office furniture is purchased for $2000.00 and has a salvage value of $800.00 and a life expectancy of 7 years, then you would be able to deduct $171.00 (rounded) in depreciation each year.

Acceleration Depreciation Method.

This depreciation method allows the business owner to take a larger depreciation in the first few years of of an asset purchase, with smaller deductions following until the end of its useful life.

Use the IRS tables in Publication 946 to figure out the deductions for your property under the Acceleration Depreciation Method. Because of its usefulness to small business when they are first starting out, it is a common method that should be closely scrutinized for maximum use.

Section 179 Expense Deduction.

This depreciation method allows you to deduct the entire cost of an asset in the year that it is acquired up to a set amount by the IRS. Refer back to the IRS publication for current depreciation allowances.

Many new small business owners simply do not understand the nuances of Depreciation, and all to often elect to ignore it during their tax filing season.

This is ultimately a bad Negative (-) dollar move.

Remember this from "Marsh's Theory of the Doubling Negative $?"

Recall that takes two (2) Positive (+) dollars, to offset a Single Negative (-) dollar.

By not taking advantage of all the deductions you are legally allowed, you are reducing the impact value for every two (2) Positive (+) dollars earned.

The US Code says:

"When a business depreciation-eligible item is sold or traded, is lost or otherwise becomes a casualty, the Accumulated Depreciation so accrued to its date of disposal will be counted as TAXABLE INCOME when calculating Long or Short Term Capital Gains or Losses, or other Ordinary Income."

Translated into Common Sense this dictates:

Count Depreciation Deductions On Annual Tax Returns

In business every dollar counts.

Learn to identify that almost everything is a resource of some kind and be sure to use every asset to its maximum allowable value.

NEVER CHEAT on your filings, always pay what you owe, but do not pay more than what you owe unless you like giving the government interest free loans.

CHAPTER
-12-

"The biggest thrill wasn't winning on Sunday,
but in meeting the payroll on Monday"

- Art Rooney

Question 8.
How are you going to conduct
Payroll and Contract Labor?

Any Professional Accountant or Bookkeeper will concur that Federal and State Payroll Processing is horribly time-consuming.

For an international operating company, payroll and taxes get even more convoluted as you will likely be dealing with one or more country tax codes interacting with each other in complex ways in addition to your native country codes.

In the Internal Revenue Service (IRS) and the State's eyes:

"W-2 Payroll Reporting/Payment is either 100% RIGHT...or 100% WRONG."

NO EXCEPTIONS.

It bears repeating from earlier chapters that in the IRS World:

"If an Employer cannot afford to pay his/her employees, and attendant Federal & State Payroll Taxes, he / she cannot afford to even be in business."

That IS Cold! But, THAT is the reality of business.

Proper accountability and payment of payroll and taxes is a critical company function you MUST get right.

There is no IRS Ombudsman that has been created yet to listen to an employer's Payroll 'Tales of Woe.' Pay what you owe, but be sure to pay only what you owe.

New business Owners need to download from the Internal Revenue Service website IRS Circular E, Publication 15, for the specific payroll year in question (https://www.irs.gov).

Study this 60+ page document closely. The first 44 pages serve as a Basic Primer for processing W-2 type payrolls.

Most pages represent the usable tables for FIT (Federal Income Tax) Withholding, depending on the Employee's Filing Status, and the number of Withholding Allowances claimed.

So what types of employees will you have to deal with for payroll?

The W-2 Employee.

IF an individual can be directed by an employer to come to a work site at a specific time, date, and workplace location, then IRS considers that person to be a W-2 Employee.

To determine the amount of FIT withholding, the Employee fills out and provides the Employer a Form W-4.

For a W-2 Employee, the Employer (or hired Payroll Service, Bookkeeper or Accountant) will deduct the Social Security FICA/ Medicare and the appropriate FIT from the Employee's Gross Paycheck.

The result is then the Payroll Net Dollar Amount due the Employee, either by separate check, or Direct Deposit.

When the Employer files the IRS Form 941 Quarterly, the Employer MATCHES only the 7.65% Social Security/Medicare amount, thereby paying 15.30% times (X) Gross Pay. Review back to the IRS official publications for current percentages.

Be aware that each State has its own Employment Commission, and may have separate laws governing its own quarterly reports/payments.

The Employee will be issued W-2 Forms by February 1, following the Calendar Year's End.

These W-2 forms (reflecting Taxable Pay, Social Security Total withhold Tax dollars; Medicare Total Pay with tax and FIT withholding dollars) are used by the Employee to file his/her own Form 1040 set Federal Individual Tax Return by April 15, following the W-2's Calendar Year.

Contractors / Sub-Contractors.

NO taxes of any kind are withheld on Contractors/Sub-Contractors employed by your business.

Contractors/Sub-Contractors each receive a Form 1099-MISC by each February 1, after the Calendar Year closes.

Each Contractors/Sub-Contractors is responsible for his/her Income Taxes and Self-Employment Taxes, since the 1099-MISC automatically triggers Solo Schedule C.

By US Code, Contractors/Sub-Contractors are NOT considered Employees.

Contractors/Sub-Contractors, generally MUST use their own tools, equipment, and/or vehicles unless specifically spelled out as provided within the scope of work of their contract.

Contractors/Sub-Contractors generally CANNOT be specifically directed by a SBO to show up for any job at a designated time, date or location.

Contractors/Sub-Contractors, generally are employed to provide a deliverables based product or service by a set time at a set of determined locations that you have contracted with them to provide for or on behalf of your company.

Typical professions using IRS-recognized Contractors/Sub-Contractors are: the Building and Construction Trade; Landscaping Services; the Entertainment Industry; and Insurance 'Storm Chasers' (casualty Insurance claims adjusters).

Recipient Contractor/Sub-contractor needs to fill out and give to the Hiring Company a Form W-9, providing his/her name, address and Social Security Number.

Aside from the above provisions, Contractors/Sub-Contractors MUST be treated as a formal W-2 Employee and may be entitled to the same rights and protections W-2 Employees may have pursuant to federal and state employment laws.

Any contractors or sub-contractors receiving $600.00 or more cumulatively in a calendar year MUST be issued a Form 1099-MISC as a mandatory payroll action. An exception to this is when the recipient is either a type of corporation, then the issuance is optional. The IRS penalty has historically increased and is never tax deductible.

The larger the number of Employees or Contractors/Sub-Contractors that your company utilizes in conducting its business, the more time you will need to devote to the administrative operations side of your business.

This management aspect of business can become very complex, very quickly, particularly in times of rapid business expansion. Do not ignore or underestimate the time this management will take or the details you will need to complete for payroll.

If you have more than three W-2 Employees, are utilizing multiple Contractors/Sub-Contractors, or are simply not proficient at payroll and tax application, it is strongly suggested that you look into procuring the services of a hired Payroll Service, Bookkeeper or Accountant.

Note that the use of these services does not alleviate you as the SBO from financial or legal obligations related to your business payroll requirements.

As the SBO the final responsibility to ensure compliance is yours.

CHAPTER
-13-

"Leadership is a privilege to better the lives of others.
It is not an opportunity to satisfy personal greed."

- Mwai Kibaki

Question 9.
Profit Margins. What is the Fair Market value of your product or service as a measure of Value Profit Margin?

One of the most important decisions for the SBO is to make sure to Price your Goods or Services fairly.

Profit is what makes your business grow and able to weather hard economic condition periods. Profit will be either reinvested in the business or banked for future needs. Note that Profit is not the same as retail Markup. Markup is what it costs to make a good or service minus what it is actually sold for.

People sometimes use the term "reasonable profit margin" which can be anywhere from 5 percent to 20 percent of the sale price of your product or services. In practice, calculating profit it is a bit more complicated.

The first thing you need to understand about profit is that it is really split into four parts, each with their own uses:

Gross Profit

Gross Profit is the calculation of the total Revenue your small business generates subtracting the total cost of expenditures.

The Revenue is any collected amount of funds during a given period of time (say like a week, month, or year). For example, say your businesses makes $1000.00 dollars as revenue to run a hot-dog stand for time period of a week:

Your direct expenses to make the hot-dogs caused you to expend $700.00 to make the number of hot-dogs to sell.

By taking your revenue of $1000.00 and subtracting your cost to make the hot-dogs at $700.00, this gives a Gross Profit of $300.00 for the week.

(Revenue $1000.00 minus $700.00 cost to make hot-dogs = $300.00)

Gross Profit Margin

Gross Profit Margin is the calculation of your Gross Profit divided by your Revenues.

From the example above to calculate your Gross Profit Margin you would take your $300.00 Gross Profit divided by your $1000.00 revenue to determine your Gross Profit Margin at 30% for that week:

($300.00/$1000.00 = .3 or 30%)

Gross Profit Margin is mainly useful to you in determining how much profit you are making on an individual product or service line. This can be used to decide if a given product or service is worth pursuing.

Net Profit

Net Profit is the calculation of your Gross Profit minus all the expenses to run your small business for a given time period.

Expenses are anything you spent during this same period to operate your business. These expenses include common things such as labor, rent, utilities, equipment, and interest loans from banks and so on.

From the example above, it takes you $700.00 to produce your hot-dogs for a week plus $100.00 to run all other costs.

Now your Net Profit is your Revenue of $1000.00 minus your Expenses at $800.00 ($700.00 + $100.00) for a Net Profit of $200.00 for the week.

Net Profit Margin

Net Profit Margin is similar to calculating your Gross Profit Margin in that you take your Net Profit and divide it by your Revenues.

This now makes your Net Profit Margin for the week your Net Profit of $200.00 divided by your Revenue of $1000.00 to equal 20%.

(Net Profit $200.00/$1000.00 = .2 or 20%)

Net Profit Margin is useful to you in determining how much profit you are making for your SBO rather than on an individual product or service line.

103

If your Net Profit Margin is too low, it is a good indicator that your business may be in some financial difficulty.

Each of the calculations can be used to adjust your profit margins to suit the given market that you are in.

Profit may be adjusted by either taking in more Revenue (adjusting the sale price of your goods or services) and by lowering your Expenses (reducing overhead cost, rental location, utilities, etc...).

As part of your determination to enter a market, you will need to run comparisons on the prices of similar goods or services and see how well you compete.

Comparing a given price for a market area you can make a good initial determination on what the maximum is you should set your sell price. By using your market data you can determine if you might take a market lead by providing that product or service for a lower price with the goal of outselling your completion.

If you are offering a new product or service in an area where it does not currently exist, you may have to experiment with prices to see what the market will bear. Generally, start low enough to be enticing, but high enough to cover your full expenses. Be careful, just as you are watching market data for insights on pricing, you can expect both customers and rival businesses will be watching your own pricing successes or setbacks.

When making adjustments to your profit, you may find that it is very easy to anger or alienate your customer base depending on what you are providing and how the value of that product or service is perceived.

Above all DO NOT GET GREEDY!

Consumers usually can spot unadulterated Greed with a Capital 'G.'

When you start your small business, you are counting on 'X' number of customers to purchase or pay at a given price that is more than the total cost of making or providing a good or service.

Now raise that price ever-so-slightly and you may be thinking you will increase your Revenue generated and both your Gross Profits and Net Profits, but instead you may see fewer people willing to pay the higher price.

Why?

Market behavior is a whole science unto itself, but in a most general sense customers are looking for the best deal they can find that balances quality and price with what they can afford.

For your customer, expect that there is some perceived price point where an even incrementally smaller price is higher than they are willing to spend on a given product or service. It is not a coincidence that may products are priced at $X.99, that next whole dollar is a deal breaker for some.

At the point where a customer has hit their price limit, they will either decide to shop elsewhere (usually to your competition) or decide they do not need what is being sold (lowering its priority in their lives).

A customer declining a purchase opportunity may be limited to a single sales type your company offers, however it can also reflect something more serious.

A critical event to avoid is leaving the impression where a customer decides (rightly or wrongly) that the way your small business operates is to gouge its customers.

When that happens your company reputation can be damaged in ways that is very hard for any business to recover from, which in turn may directly impact future sales from your entire customer base.

Unhappy customers are very quick to jump to conclusions based on even a single negative experience.

Taking Customer Service seriously is ESSENTIAL to your small business as a means to mitigate unhappy customers from damaging your company reputation.

Consider the following sanitized and simplified tale from my own catalog of experience that occurred while I was growing up in Texas that illustrates this particular point.

My local Metropolitan Transit Company bus ticket was priced at approximately $1.00/ride for a one-way trip.

In this case the Transit Company had Revenue of $100.00 for 100 patrons.

The company leadership decided to double the bus ticket rate to $2.00 thinking Revenue will increase to $200.00.

Enter the Metropolitan Transit Company's first mistake, believing there will be an increased Profit Margin and overall Net Profits.

So what happens?

That expected Revenue increase to $200.00 dollars instead only comes to $80.00.

Why?

Because only 40 total riders decide the price is worth the use of the public transport.

This of course panicked the Metropolitan Transit Company leadership due to the loss of Revenue over what they were originally making at the $1.00 a ticket fare.

Did they return fares to previous levels to lure customers back?

No.

By the company failing to understand their customer base, they instead again hiked their basic ride rate thereby ensuring a self-fulfilling prophecy of continuing diminishing Gross Revenues.

Let's just say it did not end well for that company.

But why did it end that way?

The company corporate leadership not only overvalued their own service, but believed they were actually entitled to the Revenue from low valued customers whom they believed were dependent on their service.

That company fell prey to making false assumptions.

Greed will kill your company.

Short term gains do not make for long term Revenue increases and reputation is not something that you can take from a stockpile to restore easily once it is gone. Once your reputation is damaged it, it is almost impossible to repair. Do NOT lose your reputation, guard it as you would any other company resource.

This chapter best describes the concept taught in Economics 101 as the Law of Diminishing Returns.

CHAPTER
-14-

"A successful man is one who can lay a firm foundation
with the bricks that others throw at him"

- David Brinkley

Managing Your Company Reputation

Why do you have marketing and advertising plans?

They serve a purpose besides just getting out to the public that you
have a good or service available to sell. They are a foundation on
which your company reputation is built, and therefore your company's
future.

We talked last chapter about the financial impacts of greed.

Now lets discuss that the impacts a company reputation can have.

For a start up company, you are both hindered in your initial anonymity,
but also are insulated with some level of protection.

Your company reputation is the basis of your company brand.

Your brand, regardless of what product or service you are selling is
what the customer is actually buying if they are going to be repeat
customers.

Companies that have a good reputation deal fairly with their customers, have superior products, and great customer service. That reputation continues to grow and draw in more customers, providing a cycle of growth and success you are ultimately aiming for.

A bad reputation can kill your company just as quickly as poor financial decisions can.

When you are a small and unknown company, there are not enough people who may even know about your goods or services.

Your marketing and advertising plans are designed to correct that.

Early on this relative obscurity will allow you to make some public mistakes that could become crippling later, but that anonymity will not last for long if you are building your company toward sustained growth and successes.

Recall the discussion about being financially unprepared for the price of success?

Here is the other side of the funding dilemma success may cause.

If you cannot meet market demands, you can expect two typical outcomes.

First, if you fail to deliver your product to a demanding costumer base, your buyers will complain.

Loudly

Your target customer does NOT care why THEIR order could not be fulfilled, or was summarily canceled.

The customer only CARES that they did not receive their product or service at the price they expected.

What makes a customer feel worse is if they paid ahead of time (such as a pre-order) and you do not deliver.

The customer will not only complain, they will do so with great enthusiasm because you tied up their money when they could have gotten something else instead of your product.

And if there is one thing that is easy for a customer to do, it is to complain with vigor.

It matters little in way of your explanations if they feel "cheated", whether or not they have a true basis for that perception (and if they truly do have reason to feel cheated, you have MUCH deeper problems in your company to attend to).

To a customer, perception equals reality.

In modern times it is exceedingly easy for a disgruntled customer to take to Social Media and thoughtlessly trash your small business to people who have never heard of your company and despite any facts that support the product or service you are rendering is top notch quality.

Again, perception equals reality.

Secondly when dealing customers who you fail to satisfy, you may have a customer try to threaten or take legal action against your company. Even in clear cases where a customer is guilty of outright liable against your business, you may not have enough capital set aside to devote to defending your product against malicious attacks, let alone protect or restore your reputation.

A business competitor may also try to damage your reputation to their market gain.

A truly despicable tactic of some large corporations is to sue a smaller company for some perceived threat to the larger company copyright, patent, or trademark in an effort to bankrupt the smaller company with legal fees that stretch on for civil court cases that can last for years.

The Smaller company can prevail, but even in victory its reputation may have been irreparably damaged within its targeted customer base who in turn may not (never) realize the smaller company was in the right (or care).

Reputations are almost never 100% repairable, no matter the circumstances that led to the damage or the mitigation efforts conducted.

And then there is the boon and bane of the World Wide Web (WWW) by way of the Internet. Gateway to the world, full of opportunity and it seems some quite angry people at times.

A sad reality in the unreality that is the digital world is that there are whole communities that do nothing but thrive on bad mouthing companies with little to no actionable consequences that can be taken against them. Their own anonymity protects them just as you being a small business may have protected you from the attention of larger corporations.

You cannot and should not count on buying a good reputation, which may be your prime motivator to become a Franchise Owner. Franchise Owners must remember that they are always at the mercy of the larger core corporation and if the main franchise CEO drives the core business into the ground, its your reputation that goes with it.

To build and protect your reputation, and regardless of your own internet resources and knowledge, you must maintain and be aware of your company status as secure internet presence.

In today's market you ARE your internet presence, once on the Web, negativity neither goes away nor is easily fixed.

An untended web presence for example can result in everything from a severely damaged reputation with negative impacts to sales, to an outright cuber-criminal using your company's information as a front for conducting money scam operations.

The internet enables disgruntled customers, despite likely being a small number of your client base, to use the power of social media in much the same way newspaper critics of the past did to give the perception they are a much larger majority than they are.

Always remember that customers respond to perceptions on reputations (deserved or not) and that perception does not have to equal truth.

Do not underestimate the power of the internet and electronic messaging systems. If you yourself do not understand this aspect of business – learn quickly or hire an employee versed in this sort of business skill.

Perception equals reality. See how that keeps coming up?

In all cases of reputation damage, only time and intense outlay of marketing effort will begin to undo some of the damage.

Look to the movie industry as an example of how much it takes to make a blockbuster movie truly earn back its production costs. A bad review can cost a studio millions of dollars in just damage control alone, eating into any profits.

You have a small business, and when starting up you are protected somewhat by the fact that customers do not know you and rivals are not targeting you. As a natural consequence of successful business operations, this condition will change or your company will quickly be unprofitable and fail.

Be knowledgeable, but be active.

You must take an active role in managing and promoting your company reputation.

Capitalize on a good reputation, and plan for the success you are expecting to encounter in your business plan so you can meet customer expectations. This is largely where having a good advertising campaign does double duty in not only helping to managing your company reputation or image, but also in opening up your product or services to new customers.

Plan for success, but also develop plans to deal with a bad reputation.

If you think you have a reputation damaging incident, ask yourself what steps can you take to fix or keep a reputation from suffering further damage?

The one place to start is by ensuring that your product or service is of quality and fairly priced. There are many ways to manage this, but it may mean taking a lower initial profit margin as you build your company's reputation to ensure the customers understand the value they are receiving (selling a product this way is sometimes called loss leader).

By taking a lesser profit on a quality product or service, you are building your long term customer base who will spread word of your company by mouth or reviews. As you become more successful, you can reasonably and judiciously raise your prices and work to lower or balance your expenses.

Remember that pricing your product or service too cheaply may imply a lower quality or service to some of your customers. Use your marketing plan to get to know your customers and advertise to them, building off any reputation you have positively developed.

When you see indications of a negative reaction or reputation developing, take immediate and decisive steps to correct the action and ensure that action is publicly known.

A good marketing plan may be able to offset the damage a negative reputation may inflict through shear weight of positive response. This may however be very expensive initially, requiring the services of a specialist firm and must be handled with extreme care.

One last case to consider on mitigating the impacts of a bad reputation is to somehow turn it around to make it work for you.

Take warning that this is an exceptionally difficult process and may work only in a limited number of cases.

If struck with a bad review, with the right products and marketing plans, then a negative advertisement campaign can be run based on the truism that there is no bad publicity.

Customers knowing your brand, even negatively at fist can work in your favor if you can create an opinion split and get the supporters of your business to work in your favor to try to convert naysayers. When you suddenly have a change in product that meets the perceived market outrage, you 'grant' a victory to those that worked against you turning their efforts into another means to spread the word about your products.

VERY hard to do, but not unheard of.

With a little searching you can find examples of even the most well known national chains that suffered from severe or potentially crippling negative response from a product or company action turn their luck around and use that negative reaction to propel themselves into profit.

If people are talking about your company negatively (possibly making personal attacks against you personally) you can at least realize that you have some level of the public's attention that for a short time you may be able to capitalize on.

This will likely only work for a superior product or service you that will allow you to turn bad publicity around so that your company's negative reputation become essentially satire, or even a self depreciating joke the public can join in on.

Understand this ONLY works where your product or service quality can be shown to be superior and the nature of the negativity does not cross illegal, immoral, or unethical boundaries.

As a start up small business, do not underestimate the value of your marketing plan and the resources that it will require.

If you cannot repair your reputation, consider if it is better to fold the current business, salvage what you can, and start again at Chapter-1.

CHAPTER
-15-

"This is not the end. It is not even the beginning of the end. But it is perhaps, the end of the beginning."

- Winston Churchill

Tying It All Together.

Having read and completed the chapter exercises you now have enough information about the various planning requirements required to start or refine your small business. Now that you know what type of business service or product you plan to provide, take your worked SBO Startup answers through the following business checks:

Select your Business Name

The company name should be easily pronounce and should be appropriate for your business type. The name may represent something real or fictitious when it is registered. The main thing however is to make sure it is not already taken or trademarked prior to applying for your business registration or federal EIN. Check with your state agency registration to see if the name you want is already taken. To check if the business name is Trademarked, go to the U.S. Patent and Trademark Office (USPTO) at www.ustpo.gov.

Write a preliminary Business Plan

Take your time to write out a simple business plan. For more extensive business plans consider using any number of readily available software.

In context for this book, your business plan should include the following:

Business Executive Summary

Write out your bottom line what your company is going to be providing and what your endstate goal is. This should be around a page and should include your overall strategic market placement intent and capture your overall Dynamic Vision for your company.

Business Description

Detail what your company provides, what specific industry market you intend to do business in, and what type of service or product will be specifically provided.

Determine overhead costs

This includes everything to run and operate your business that will cost you money. Be sure to include things such as development costs, licensing, and testing fees. Be sure to be as detailed on this as you can, it will directly impact your

Marketing and Competition Summary

Write down details about who your customers are and where you will conduct your business (fixed physical locations, area service, online, and so on). At this stage also create your initial Product Sales Marketing Plan that details how your product is going to be advertised to your intended customers, keeping in mind that you may attract additional sales demographics that are not your primary sales focus. Create your new business cards and other advertising and marketing materials.

At this point your should also set up your Internet Web Site which not only provides you marketing space, but do not activate any credit card processing services for point-of-sales until you have your invoices created and your business banking account set up. This is the start of where you begin to manage your company's reputation.

Startup Capitalization Funding

Determine how much capital funding you need for your business startup funds. Start by adding up all your anticipated cost outlays for the next 3 years with an additional reserve for the unexpected.

Concept of Operations (CONOPS)

Write how your business actually is going to be run day to day, by who, and how your product or service gets to the customer, and how you collect payment. A good draft outline for a typical day detailing activities opening to closing and a monthly overview of key business dependencies (i.e. if a retail shop, what are the restock days) needed work through is a good start.

Select your Business Structure

Choose from sole proprietorship, partnership, limited liability company (LLC), or Corporation (Remember in the USA ONLY the IRS can grant S-type corporation approval). Once you have determined your business structure, apply for 'For-Profit Entity Corporation" status from your State Secretary of State (SOS), or its equivalent. These Franchise Application Fees vary from-state-to-state. Once approval documents are received, you now own your new small business. Be sure to have a full understanding of all legal requirements, protections, and liabilities for your business. Be sure that you fully understand and research any state and federal tax requirements prior to applying for your business structure.

Obtain your Federal EIN
(Employer Identification Number)

Once you receive your SOS Original Documents, you need a free IRS EIN to conduct your business. In the United States you will do this online at the IRS website www.irs.gov.

You will be guided through a series of questions to determine your eligibility for an EIN. Once you 'pass-this-test', the web site will ask how you want to receive your Official IRS EIN Approval Letter. If you elected to Start-up as an LLC and your LLC has more than one (1) Member, the IRS EIN Letter will automatically dictate your entity as a Form 1065, US Partnership Corporation complete with an extra 15.30% of Self Employment Taxes for each Partner Member.

As of this printing edition, there are two options for receiving your EIN Approval Letter. The first is to have the approval letter mailed to you by United States Postal Service (USPS). Use a well trusted mail receiving address if choosing this option. This address does not have to be at your place of business.

The second option is to print the EIN Approval Letter out from your home or office computer in "Portrait" format. Always print in portrait mode and not landscape mode to ensure it prints correctly. If you choose this print option, make sure your printer works (plugged-in, paper, toner/ink).

It is recommended that you print both a physical copy and a PDF copy for your use. Save the PDF copy, and/or scan your physical copy to keep a digital file on hand for your records.

Why is this important to understand?

You only get ONE crack at printing this out...as the warning-on-the-web-site-screen informs you. Remember that you need this form to open your business checking account!

The IRS neither keeps EIN Approval Letters on file, nor provides ANY means to replace the Original issue information number.

If the web site computer THINKS you have printed the Approval Letter, it also assumes the letter was printed...whether or not you successfully did so.

Capitalization Funding Acquisition

Now that you have your Banking Business Account, arrange for or gather your Capital Startup Funds in whatever primary currency you will be doing business with your bank with.

This may range from personal funds you have raised and can risk losing to bank loans. Make sure that the funding is accessible and that only authorized members of your business has access to expend it.

Set up your business Operations

Refer to your business plan to set up your business location, acquisition of administrative equipment and furniture, and all other items required to run the business according to your CONOPS. Specific items to pay attention to are your Business Location, Manufacturing process and or suppliers, Product Inventory management and Storage, and administrative requirements such as your business standard operating procedures (SOP). The SOP is the written implementation of your CONOPS that documents details for your day to day business operations and management of policies. It includes things such as how the business conducts sales to how personnel benefits or discipline is conducted.

Business Checking Account

Take your Original copy of your SOS entity approval documents and your IRS EIN Approval Letter to the bank or credit union of your choice. In many States, these documents are required under State Law for a Business Checking Account creation.

State Sales and Use Tax Account

Set up a sales and use tax account by going to www.eftps.gov to set up your account, where you will provide your Business Checking account just ONCE for future debit deposits or payments. Inquire from the State Comptroller or Sales Tax Collection equivalent in YOUR state as to whether or not your Products Sold, or Services Rendered, are subject to a Sales and Use Tax Report (Monthly or Quarterly) and/or Sales Tax Collection and subsequent payment unless selling to a Tax-Exempt customer (churches, non-profits, etc).

Select the Business Accounting Method Type

Your New Business must select which of the two (2) basic types of accounting it wants to employ during the course of its operations.

These are Cash and Accrual:

Cash. The most commonly used method for a Home Office-based business. This method means that ALL Income AND Expenses are counted in the Tax Year in which their transactions occur.

Accrual. This method is preferred and used by almost all larger businesses. This accounting method centers around the 'Intent' or 'Obligation' of the income or expenses.

Income example. Accounts Receivables are invoices prepared in one Tax Year, but may not actually be paid until later. This income counts as income for the Tax Year the Invoice or Statement was issued to your Buyers.

Expenses Example. If a business intends or obligates expenses for supplies, the resale of product, purchase of office furniture and furnishings, electronics, office computers or other equipment, building improvements (you OWN the property) or leasehold improvements (you LEASE the property) then these expenses can be counted in the Tax Year for which contracted, regardless of when these expenses are actually paid.

This includes payment via credit card, store credit from a vendor, cash, check or money order.

Refer to your business plan CONOPS to guide you in what type of Accounting Method you should use. For some business, regular third party auditing may be a requirement and the retention of an accounting service may be an additional administrative expense to plan for.

Obtain Business License and Permits

Before embarking on your first sales you need to ensure you are not breaking State, Federal, or possibly International Laws. You will need to verify with your individual state to ensure you are meeting all your legal requirements to run your business.

Some of the permits you have already acquired in setting up your busies operations include your Federal EIN and registering your DBA. Other licenses and permits you may need include Location Based Permits:

Zoning and Land Use permits. Mainly in cases of new manufacturing businesses and some home business cases.

Health Department Permit. Most often a requirement for the preparation and sale of food.

Fire Department Permit. May be required for certain manufacturing business and for most businesses that have a large amount of customers on premises such as a gym, restaurant, or nightclub.

State Tax License. Used for the sale of most products or services you plan to sell. This includes online businesses where you will need to abide by the state in which your website business is run from (generally a license is not a requirement for each state you sell to).

Special Sales Permits at the State and County levels within the USA include the selling of liquor, Lottery tickets, gasoline/petrol, and firearms.

Some business sales require State or Federal Business License or Permits which include:

Broadcasting Services License. See the Federal Communications Commission for permitting details at www.FCC.gov. Note that there are different licenses required for community radio, public radio, and television that differ significantly within and outside the United States. Some broadcasting requirements are still evolving, with internet radio license downloadable sound (POD Casting) or video subject to emerging regulation while still largely in an unregulated state.

Special consideration should be given to the legal requirements and compliance with the Digital Millennium Copyright Act of 1998.

Investment Consulting/Advising. U.S. Securities and Exchange Commission issues permits Per SEC mission statement at www.SEC.gov, the SEC was formed "to protect investors, maintain fair, orderly and efficient markets, and facilitate capital formation." This includes many licensing and permitting requirements compliance with public law in both a physical and online only environment.

Import and Export License. You will need a Company Identification Number (CIN) and register with the U.S. Department of Commerce at www.usa.gov and the U.S. Customs and Border Protection (CBP) at www.CBP.gov.

Meat Products, Pharmaceuticals, or Drug Manufacture.
See the U.S. Food and Drug Administration requirements at www.FDA.gov.

State/Interstate Good Transportation. See the U.S. Department of Transportation requirements at www.transportation.gov.

Manufacture and sale of alcohol, tobacco, and firearms.
See the U.S. Bureau of Alcohol, Tobacco, and Firearms for specific details at www.ATF.gov.

Other permits or manufacturing marks may need to be obtained for both marketing or legal protection reasons as well as ensuring compliance with regulatory agencies. Two of the most import for manufacturing and retail sales businesses include (but are in no way limited to):

Occupation Safety and Health Administration (OSHA).
This agency under the U.S. Department of Labor assures safe and healthful working conditions for working men and women by setting and enforcing standards and by providing training, outreach, education and assistance. Compliance with OSHA regulations is applicable to nearly all business types, including the penalties for non-compliance. See www.OSHA.gov for detailed requirements.

Electronics manufacturing and life safety. The Underwriters Laboratories (UL) provides safety certification, testing, inspection, and training for electronic devices and material components. See requirements located at www.UL.com. Note that this is one of the authorized companies allowed to perform safety testing by OSHA.

Copyright Registration or License. Formal copyright registration may be needed to secure authors and inventors exclusive rights to their respective writings and discoveries. More information on registering your business original works can be found at www.copyright.gov.

If you are creating or selling a product that is owned by another individual or business entity you will need to obtain and pay for the use of that copyright.

Patent and Trademark Registration or License. Your business plan should specify the importance of any trademarks or patents required for your business operations. Detailed information can be found at the U.S. Patent and Trademark Office at www.USPTO.gov.

If you are creating or selling a product or service that is already Trademarked or Patented by another business entity or individual you will need to obtain a license and pay for the use of that trademark or patent.

Failure to obtain and correctly utilize a license, permit, or registration may incur severe legal issues carrying both professional and personal liabilities.

It is highly advisable to apply this checklist for an online business just as if it were a physical location business in order to minimize chances of legal oversights.

Legal Services Plan

Due to potential copyright, trademark, legal permit filing, or legal defense requirements, your CONOPS and SOP should address how your company deals with legal complications. This may mean the requirement to retain on-staff lawyers or hiring of legal representation.

Selling Your Product or Service

Now that you have the above set up, its time to start offering your product or service.

One of the key checks here is to ensure you have your product or service available in sufficient quantities to meet your market requirements and the means to ensure distribution to your customers.

From your CONOPS, understand if you maintain your own Inventory Stock of Cost-of-Goods-Sold (COGS) or are running a process by which you funnel your inbound orders to specific vendors. Your corporation pays THEM, but they ship directly to YOUR Customer.

If providing a service, this is where you ensure the administrative details such ensuring your employees are licensed and bonded properly and are equipped to perform the service to be provided.

New Beginnings

If you are able answer all of the above business checklist and are able to comply with all licensing, permitting, regulatory and legal compliance requirements while having enough Startup Capital Funding (including a reasonable reserve) and business plan that takes into account competition and expansion, you have successfully taken into account and mitigated the primary pitfalls encountered by the SBO and passed the first milestone for starting your own small business!

Congratulations!

This is a significant accomplishment and milestone.

Now go out there and make your mark on the world of business, but in the competitive business world be sure to keep your eyes on the future's horizon.

Always remember that businesses is constant work, but good business outcomes happen because of owners who plan good business.

No more than three years from answering this checklist, go back and do it all again.

CHAPTER
-16-

"Education is when you read the fine print.
Experience is what you get if you don't."

- Pete Seeger

Recognizing Business Pitfalls.

Now that you have completed your initial business planning for your small business, it is time to run a check on your planning to see if you are headed toward avoidable business Pitfalls.

Starting with the definition of Pitfall from the Merriam-Webster Dictionary:

Pitfall (noun | pit-fall)

1: Trap, Snare; specifically: a pit flimsily covered or camouflage and used to capture and hold animals or men.

2: A hidden or not easily recognized danger or difficulty.

This definition allows us to see the context of the danger a pitfall of some kind may have.

Using what you know for your new business frame of reference, lets expand this definition to the context of this book in an effort to define a Business Pitfall.

Business Pitfall (noun | bus-in-ess pit-fall)

1: A hidden, unrecognized, or unresolved planning or financial requirement that severely impacts a business available resources or existence.

2: A commonly encountered business scenario that is underestimated or not planned for due improper priority listing.

3: An avoidable business decision resulting in a negative outcome.

The first Business Pitfall you need to check the answer for is:

Who is in charge of your company?

Any answer other than "I Am" or a well defined "We Are" likely means you already have a management problem you need to fix.

In a business partnership there should be a clearly defined business hierarchy or chain of command empowered to make decisions and commit company resources.

No matter if the commitment of company resources is delegated to a subordinate manager, the responsibility for the company ALWAYS rests with the owner (partnership or not).

When legal or code penalties are enacted however, you can count on the legal system making exceptionally clear who is considered responsible.

This is one of the main reasons why going into business with a friend or business partner is not recommended. Any confusion over who is in charge will impact making business decisions, placing the company at risk.

As per the IRS, a Tax Matters Person (TMP) will be named on the partnership tax return From 1065 to respond to any questions involving Federal Tax questions as concerns the partnership.

The second Business Pitfall you need to check the answer for:

Are you spending more time working in the business than on the business?

To become successful as an SBO, you can throw the notion of a 35 to 40 hour work week right out the window. Your work hours now consist of whatever time it takes to make your business a success.

You need to clearly understand that the activities of producing goods or services is not your 'job', it is running the business itself. The 'boring stuff' or payroll, taxes, paying rent, and managing employees is the heart of your business success, not you doing all the work.

If you are spending the majority of your time creating products yourself or providing a time consuming service, you are likely neglecting the business operations details you outlined in the Business Plan CONOPS or SOP.

Those documents are important because they tell you what must be done to make your business function. If the CONOPS or SOP is not being followed and there is no negative business impact, then they need to be revised to eliminate unneeded policies or procedures that waste time or resources.

This second general Business Pitfall should cause you to pause to reflect on whether you really want a business or not. This concept was covered extensively in the previous chapter exercises, but take time to consider again why you are wanting to run a business providing your goods or services rather than working for someone else doing the same.

Having a great idea for a product or service is NEVER enough. All the hard work comes from the business operation details that WILL make or break your small business.

The third general Business Pitfall to check for:

Are you emotionally mature and ready for the stress to handle running a business?

This is your small business (and maybe someday your large company) and you can fully expect some business peaks and valleys to occur which can cause a yo-yo effect occasionally known as the "Business Blues".

It is entirely understandable and expected that you will invest significant time and resources in your small business, but you will also invest significant emotional attachment that will cause a great deal of stress.

The idiom "Its not personal, its business" applies to how you can expect to be treated by customers or business partners (internal and external), but it does not apply to your own view of your company.

This company is your idea, your product, your service that you may be relying on for the livelihood of yourself or family.

You business may be a source of intense pride and or accomplishment, particularly if it is meant to passed on to family.

This business is in fact nothing but personal to you, even if its just a means as a stepping stone to something else.

It has value to you, and that means it's a source of direct stress and emotional investment. Understand that concept and embrace it. Stress with this sort of emotional attachment can make every company setback feel like a personal failure.

People do not like to fail.

No one gets into business to fail.

You do not not want to become an SBO with the goal to fail.

Since you do not have the intention going into this business to fail, when setbacks occur, if you are not equipped with emotional maturity and the ability to deal with stress, then you should strongly reconsider starting or continuing this small business before you commit valuable time and resources to it. BUSINESS-IS BUSINESS.

Harsh, but better to know now if you are ready or not to be an SBO.

Before you get caught up in the somewhat negative discussion on the Business Blues, just know that by running through the admittedly hard truths you have encountered in this book, it is making you think about how to make better business decisions geared toward success.

You are now armed with information, and information means you can act.

As Sir Francis Bacon wrote in his 1597 publication "Meditations Sacrae and Human Philosophy" truly "Knowledge is Power".

The Business Blues of course are really just signs of potential Business Pitfalls, and one way of dealing with the blues is by embracing your job as the SBO to anticipate, recognize, and solve those pitfall challenges before they damage your company resources.

If you can take the knowledge you have learned so far in our discussions, you can harness that power to work for you.

Business Pitfalls occur commonly to new and ongoing businesses and will do so repeatedly over time.

Take the previously completed exercise notes and any developed business plans and check them to see if you can recognize any of the following **Business Pitfalls (BP)**:

BP-1. A shortage of Capitalization Cash Flow Funds. Again it literally "takes money to make money", both to start your business and to run your business. Knowing this, always maintain a firm accounting of your available cash flow.

BP-2. Do you have a shortage (or overage) of employees or contractors? Having too few, particularly skilled labor, impacts your production or service capacity negatively. Having too many is bleeding your profit and could sink your business. Balancing resources with market demand and your company capacity is critical.

BP-3. Do you have a Shortage of COGS Product? This is especially common with late shipments or stalled production from suppliers.

BP-4. A Shortage of time to provide business goods or services or to conduct business operation requirements.

BP-5. A Shortage of Paying Customers or Clients. Is it the market demographics you are in, competition, or your product or advertisement?

BP-6. Do you have Late paying Customers or Clients? You need to find out why and how to fix immediately. Customers who do not pay are receiving benefits at zero percent interest. Time is money, so time taken to get individuals or business entities to pay may impact your own bills and certainly your bottom line.

BP-7. Do you have Uncollectable Debts accrued? This is lost income, possibly with small offsets from possible tax write-offs, but will not be 100%.

BP-8. Employees and/or Personal sickness, illness, or family crisis (themselves or dependents requiring looking after) taking time away from the business. Life happens, it is messy and will take time away from your business, have a plan in your CONOPS to address this scenario and administrative business processes in place to address them (Example: know if you are legally required to provide an employee maternity/paternity leave, and then have that requirement detailed in your SOP with how that requirement will be administered).

BP-9. Physical damages involving necessary repairs or spoilage. Common occurrence in farming produce and food-industries.

BP-10. Business Expansion via franchising, or opening a second location. Expanding too fast may deplete funds/resource, saturate a market, or lead to a competitor with a similar product or service. Failure to expand may mean opportunity loss or a competitor boxing you out of paying customers.

BP-11. Use of the word or phrase "I'm Busy" with a client, friend or employee: The very word carries a very negative connotation, with far more devastating consequences such as a loss of a potential customer or client, vendor or business transaction.

BP-12. Hiring or investment with a friend. Impossible to fire, like getting caught in quicksand. Often used to gain initial Capitalization Funds, but often done without regard to long term consequences to the business particularly if that friend decides they are in charge or you owe them more than their investment. If you go into business with a friend, understand that you will likely lose them as a friend and it invites risk to the long term prospects of your company. You can somewhat mitigate impacts by having a clearly defined Business Plan with highly detailed and notarized legal documents to support your business roles.

Highly recommend having a lawyer on retainer, particularly if the initial investment friend dies or sells their company stake and you are dealing with a new party that is not your friend.

BP-13. Starting a business that may prove beyond your monetary means or physical capabilities. (Example: you buy a 'T-shirt screening machine for $10,000.00. You market your product on the internet. You receive orders for 1,000 custom T-shirts. Your SBO reputation is destroyed forever when you cannot deliver). Always look 'over-the-horizon,' to plan ahead with a firm understanding of your company capabilities and capacity.

BP-14. Opening your small business in close proximity to a similar business with a well defined market demographic. Example: Opening a Gourmet Pizza Restaurant within a 1-2 mile radius of another Gourmet Pizza Restaurant with a static population. Competition for limited paying customers may put BOTH of you out-of-business.

BP-15. Are you paying greater than 50% of your Gross Income in personnel and payroll taxes? If you are, the available Profit Margin is not sustainable.

BP-16. Is there adequate Liability Insurance Coverage for your office, storefront, Home Office or vehicle? If you are involved in a 'Liability Producing Event' the Plaintiff's Lawyer usually may well start at trying to get them a high compensation amount. Why? The plaintiff's lawyer receives 30%-40% off the top in any In court judgment or out of court settlement. Most likely your insurance company will not financially back you once your deductible coverage with them is reached. Your Solo small business Schedule-C, Rental Schedule-E or Ranch/Farm Schedule-F needs to be covered by an up-to $40,000,000.00 Limited Liability Company entity status from your Home State. This is why filing your company as a business entity as a corporation is so critically important as it helps to protect some (but not all depending on the liability type) of your personal assets.

136

BP-17. Are you taking free or un-vetted business advice? Business is exceptionally complex with many variables, but it is also highly researchable when it comes to citing where information comes from or how it is meant to be interpreted. People often talk about more than what they actually know or remember, particularly it seems outside their expertise or experience! You may know this a 'water-cooler talk', but in the Army we called them 'Barracks Lawyers'. Beware of people who dispense free advice, as it often turns out to be quite costly when faithfully followed without prior research on your part. Make sure any information you use to make a business decision is accurate and timely from someone who knows what they are talking about. Then re-check that information from at least two other sources if possible before fallowing any advice leading to a business decision. A common example I use: Would I hire a plumber to do MY open heart surgery? No offense intended to plumbers.

BP-18. Do you have access to business legal counsel? If you do not have a retained lawyer vetted in business law, make sure you understand where to acquire one and be prepared for the financial costs of use of that service. Failure to research legal liabilities is a sure route to business failure. One tactic a large corporation may take against you is to throw so many legal challenges at you that you go bankrupt defending your company in court. Understand, you may be perfectly in the right, but a business rival that preys on on other businesses can sink you if you are not extremely diligent in registering your business assets (copyrights, trademarks, patents, etc...).

BP-19. Is your Business Plan starting to make you Net Profits (Net Earnings for corporations)?

BP-20. What is your measuring stick in dollar amounts?

BP-21. Is your marketing plan working?

BP-22. Does your prospective clientele know who, or where, you even are?

BP-23. How effective has your website been in attracting sales?

BP-24. Is your Financial Plan working?

BP-25. Do your Business Plans, CONOPS, or SOPs need reassessment, refining, re-writing, or just tweaking to insure maximum utilization for the dollar?

BP-26. Have you quantified your marketing and advertising dollars, so as to truly gauge their effectiveness (more bang-for-the-buck

BP-27. Have you thoroughly vetted or investigated the certified public accountant (CPA), bookkeeper, or tax preparer you are doing business with?

Your job as the SBO is to protect and run your business in order to make YOUR money. To do so you may have determined from the exercises or active business experience that you may need the assistance of a retained service provider,

A retained service providers job is to provide a set business service, but they get paid whether or not your business succeeds as long as they do their job within the legal requirements they are bound by.

But how do you know if they are any good?

Checking Out the Help.

Service providers have reputations just like any other business owner (you in fact may be a service provider). You can look them up, but be sure to research closely who is vetting the reviews (both positive and negative) before making a decision on their use.

The most likely reason an SBO will utilize retained services is to fill critical knowledge gaps and these tend to be areas of specialization the SBO may have the least familiarity will when first setting up their small businesses such as the Bookkeeper, accountant, CPA, or tax preparer.

So how do you know if you should hire them once you have identified a need?

IF your prospective Bookkeeper, accountant, CPA, or tax preparer professional cannot satisfactorily answer the following business and legal professional questions, then DO NOT HIRE them because they do not know YOUR business well enough to help YOU.

Have them answer the following questions as appropriate to the service provided:

Does their full service Payroll Processing include and meet both Federal and State compliance?

Is a States Sales and Use Tax Report Processing & Payment offered?

Can they accurately explain the different types of business entity options, benefits, and liabilities to you?

Do they know how to conduct IRS-approved legally cross-feed Net Income/Net Earnings between your Individual Form 1040, Schedules-C, D, or F with your business entity?

Can they demonstrate they know the filing process required for documentation for a US Partnership or either type of US Corporation ('C' or 'S' types) using the 'Cash Nominee Paid/Cash Nominee Received' legal profits transference?

Can they accurately explain the true meaning and significance of the IRS' "Law of Intent?"

Do they exercise Due Diligence with regards to all facets of your small business?

Can they explain the benefits and liabilities of YOUR specific type of business, and how it is uniquely different from any other similar/dissimilar businesses as it relates to the basic economic Law of Diminishing Returns?

Do they understand, can accurately explain, and practice the Economic "Rule of 72"?

Do they understand the Theory of the Doubling Negative Dollar when you explain it to them?

Mitigating Business Pitfalls

The included list of commonly occurring Business Pitfalls checks is not remotely all-inclusive, and merely illustrates known common scenarios that you as the SBO must rise to the task of solving.

Each Business Pitfall represents a critical threat to your business that will not solve itself (unless you count going out of business as an acceptable resolution).

You are the key to mitigating your SBO Business Pitfalls.

You must understand is that while a single Business Pitfall may be encountered, mitigated, or avoided, it may in turn lead to other Business Pitfalls both on and off this list.

Avoiding and resolving Businesses Pitfalls is a recurring activity you can count on for the life of the business.

The SBO is the Boss, and when it comes to making the important business decisions that means the buck stops with you.

As the SBO, you must either recognize and solve the problem yourself, or delegate authority to commit company resources to an Office Manager, Project Manager, or hired outside agency.

For example, as the SBO you might hire an Office Manager to oversee the company's website productivity or you might reach out to a department store to help sell your products to a broader range of customers.

A common Business Pitfall mentioned above for a successful business is need for rapid business growth or expansion. This scenario often creates not only a need for additional company resources, but also the need to delegate more authority to other employees or an outside agency to keep your business moving forward. It also generally means a loss of direct control over every business decision for the company previously made by the SBO.

Span-of-control is a military term we will apply to your small business. The term is defined as the number of individuals that you as a leader can effectively manage. For the SBO, this is the number of employees you can effectively manage in the course of running your business.

An SBO's span-of-control will vary greatly based on training, experience, and business circumstances.

Depending on your type of small business, you may need to manage multiple people, particularly if your business expands at a rapid rate. This will resulting in appointing employees to act as managers themselves which can be a frustrating, if necessary requirement.

Having a clearly defined business vision, goals, and SOPs matched to clearly articulated Dynamic Vision and employee training program becomes necessary to ensure your employees and subordinate managers follow and understand your business intent.

Ultimately, the SBO as a one-person manager simply cannot be everywhere at all times for some business models.

For example a restaurant owner's span-of-control includes the chef, meal preparation crew, dining room manager, and office manager. The dining room manager's span of control would include the servers and bussers.

You as the SBO should not be out on the dinning floor trying to manage seating or cleanup, that is a job for the dining room manager. If you as the SBO try to micromanage everything yourself, you will have customers that are unhappy due to customer perceived poor service and your business may suffer, perhaps irrevocably.

The SBO's job in this case is to manage everyone by training their subordinates in the business CONOPS and SOP and providing guidance and direction for when things go wrong.

If you empower employees with the ability to make business decisions, understand you are empowering them to commit company resources and enter into legal obligations.

A retail store floor manager is usually empowered to make restocking orders. This commits money and a contract between your company and the retail goods provider.

If your manager does not have set limitations, this could lead to incurring a financial debt through over commitment of funds or purchasing the wrong items for resale. Training and managing managers is a critical skill for growing businesses.

In today's fast-paced market place, a crucial Business Pitfall to avoid is hiring the wrong employee. This could be the mistake of hiring the person with the incorrect skilleset to the accidental outright hiring of criminal elements.

Beware the temptation to hire a friend or a friend's relative (the son or daughter hire), as it follows the same pitfalls as entering into a business relationship with said friend. If you do hire a friend's relative, make sure its in a tightly controlled job that has very clearly responsibilities so if the need to let them go becomes necessary it can be done with as little hard feelings as possible.

Learn how to weed out the bad apples BEFORE hiring them.

Asking the right questions such employment experience, customer service skills, technical knowledge will create a better sphere for you as the Boss to know if these people are the right FIT for your business.

Try to ascertain what their motives are for working for you?

How will they help achieve your ultimate business endstate goals?

What are their strengths and weaknesses and loyalty to your business?

What is their reliability in showing up for work?

A single bad apple can poison your entire workforce and workplace. With all the challenges of employees, the Business Pitfall then is really determining how well can you as the SBO delegate authority?

That all depends on your management style, your skills, and your willingness to learn what you need to do to run a successful business.

It also means knowing that taking care of yourself needs to become a priority.

The single biggest Business Pitfall most small business owners make is not taking care of themselves. Physically, emotionally, and mentally.

I have heard it said:

"If you do not feel sorry for yourself, no one else will."

Well this line of thinking is a recipe for disaster as a SBO.

You want to project a truly positive attitude in your employees and their working environment. You must lead the charge into battle by managing a good work/life balance!

You need to recharge your batteries and get proper rest, lest fatigue or illness set in that robs you of time needed to spend on your business. Reserve Family Time, take a vacation, or simply unwind for a day. All of these options are attainable by a good span of control and a positive attitude.

A Prime Directive of being a business owner is to enjoy the business and take relish in the moment. Making sure your reputation is built on the highest degree of trust and dependability. Together this winning combination goes a long way to beat the Business Blues.

A positive attitude feeds positive people…which feeds positive productivity…and over the horizon your business endstate gets a lot closer.

Lastly, do not fear your own business success!

Do not be afraid to make your business so dependable and consistent in its operational running, that customers/clients/patients take you and your endeavors for granted. In other words, make your product sold or services provided the "Go-To" business for your patrons.

Years ago when asked what type of appliances they had in their kitchen, many usually responded with having a Frigidaire™, which they closely correlated to them as a 'fridge' or a refrigerator.

Why?

It was the first self-contained refrigerator invented in 1916. That model became so necessary to daily living due to its reliability to safely store food that it became the iconic brand, so iconic that any brand of refrigerator is still generally referred to as a fridge.

Word of mouth then becomes your best means of attracting and maintaining a customer base needed to successfully run your business. THAT is a Business Go-To model you ultimately want to achieve, representing both consistency dependability.

The last Business Pitfall check you need to ask yourself is how your business is being perceived.

Recall that managing your business reputation is critical to your business success. The very worse thing that can be said about any business:

Its Main Consistency Is Its Inconsistency And Dependability In Delivering Product Or Service

If this is what your company is known for, fix it immediately or expect your business to stagnate and likely fail.

145

Luck, fortune, or fate has little to do with running a business.

You as the SBO will constantly be on the lookout for Business Pitfalls to identify them and work to resolve them.

If you have the passion, desire, and skill to provide to customers a quality product or service, then its time to work the exercises in this book and begin to make your Dynamic Vision a business reality.

You are now armed with knowledge on how to recognize and mitigate the most common Business Pitfalls you are likely to encounter.

Now its up to you,

Go be your own Boss.

SBO Startup Questions

Question 1.   Why are you starting up your own business?

Question 2.   What type of business are you starting (or have)?

Question 3.   What Type of business entity will your small business
be classified as?

Question 4.   Capitalization. How will you fund your New Startup
Small Business?

Question 5.   Location. Where will you conduct business from?

Question 6.   Record-Keeping. How are you going to keep records?

Question 7.   Depreciation. How can you defray overhead costs?

Question 8.   How are you going to conduct Payroll and Contract
Labor?

Question 9.   Profit Margins. What is the Fair Market value of your
product or service as a measure of Value Profit Margin?

GLOSSARY

Explanations of Terms

Accrual Accounting Method. Business Income or Expenses are counted for Tax Returns in the Tax Year for which obligated, not when invoices or expenses are actually paid.

A/P. Accounts Payable. What the Small Business OWES a Vendor. Includes product, supplies, and services not yet paid.

A/R. Accounts Receivable. What the Small Business receives as Income for Cost-of-Goods-Sold (COGS) for product or services invoices not yet paid.

ATF. Alcohol, Tobacco and Firearms government office www.ATF. gov.

Bottom Line. Business Net Profit for Cash Flow Dollars.

Business Plan. Your Business 'Roadmap' to success. Business Plan should include a Financial Plan and a Marketing Plan.

Cash Accounting Method. All Business Income or Expenses are counted for Income Tax Return purposes in the exact Tax Year the actions were transacted. In the United States this MUST be completed by December 31.

Cash Flow. This is your readily available funds/capital to pay all A/P expenses invoices due, payroll (if any), payroll taxes (if any), Sales & Use Taxes (if applicable) and YOURSELF as Living Expenses.

149

CIP. Company Identification Number. Required for most import/export company operations.

CONOPS. Concept of Operations. This is a written document that outlines how your business runs and should be part of your business plan. It should include the small business goals or endstate as a guiding principle.

Contractor. A non-employee receiving reimbursement and a Form 1099-Miscellaneous if > $600.00 is paid in a Payroll Calendar Year (as of this publication). The Hiring Employer withholds NO taxes of any sort, making the Contractor responsible for his/her own income taxes & self-employment taxes on his/her own Schedule C.

COGS. Cost-of-Goods-Sold. A product bought wholesale, specifically for Retail Resell.

Contract Obligation. What you are legally obligated to pay for that may include leases/rental payments, utilities, COGS Product from Vendors, legal and other professional accounting or consultation fees, marketing & advertising services and so on.

CPA. Certified Public Accountant.

DBA. Doing Business As. This is a trade name of a company that may be named after individuals or entirely fictitious. Note that a DBA is the registered business name for the company and might be trademarked.

Dynamic Visionary. Someone able and willing to see in advance problems and opportunities in order to manage risk and avoid making the most frequent business mistakes.

EFTPS. Electronic Federal Tax Payment System. In the United States of America this is run by the Internal Revenue Service (IRS).

EIN. Employer Identification Number. This business number is only issued by the Internal Revenue Service.

Employee. A Business employee who has as of this publication a Social Security (6.2%), Medicare (1.45%) payroll taxes and Federal Income Taxes (FIT) deducted from each paycheck. The Business then matches ONLY the combined Social Security/Medicare Taxes withheld and sends to the IRS for payment, quarterly, monthly or weekly, depending on total Gross Payroll. Employees will be issued a Form W-2 for the Payroll Calendar Year.

FDA. U.S. Food & Drug Administration found at www.FDA.gov.

Financial Reports. This business report is gained from your accounting or bookkeeping program or service. A basic Financial Report consists of:

1. Balance Sheet. Broken down into Assets & Liabilities.
2. Profit/Loss Statement. Rather self-explanatory.
3. Accountant's Trial Balance. Shows money for ALL Business Activities.

IPO. Initial Public Offering. This business condition is triggered when a corporation goes 'Public,' and sells stock shares.

IRS. The Internal Revenue Service in the United States of America. Also, sometimes referred to as 'The Agency' in business circles.

Marketing. This is the act of buying or selling within a market and is the sum total of all the required activities necessary for the seller of a product or service to a buyer.

Markup. Represents the Business' increase in purchase price to account for overhead & profit.

Net Profit. The 'Net Earnings' for a corporation;. This is 'Ordinary Business Income,' for a partnership. It represents the Business Net Bottom Line of your net cash flow and is your Taxable Income.

OSHA. Occupation Safety and Health Administration. See www.OSHA.gov.

Overhead. The Business periodic (weekly/monthly/quarterly/yearly) expenses that include, but is not limited to rent, insurance, payroll, contractors, commissions, and utilities.

POP/POS. Point-of-Purchase or Point-of-Sale. This represents the time/place where a wholesale or retail transaction is completed.

Retail. Product bought and resold, after the Business' markup.

SBA. Small Business Administration. A local, state, or federal organization that backs small business financial loans.

SBO. Small Business Owner. You.

SE. Self-Employment, herein primary referenced for SE Taxes for Schedules C and F, Form 1040 and Form 1065.

SEC. U.S. Securities & Exchange Commission
SOP. Standard Operating Procedures. This is the written implementation of your CONOPS that documents details for your day to day business operations and management of policies.

TMP. Tax Matters Person.

TIN. Taxpayer's Identification Number, such as an EIN or Social Security Number.

UL. Underwriters Laboratory www.UL.com.

US. United States. Often used to abbreviate United States Legal Codes.

USPS. United States Postal Service.

USPTO. U.S. Patent and Trademark Office www.ustpo.gov .

Author's Biography

A Fort Worth Texas born native, Nelson L. Marsh holds a BA in Marketing from Texas Christian University, Fort Worth Texas (1959), and an LLB from the LaSalle Extension University, Chicago, Illinois (1973). He is a graduate of multiple military schools including the United States National War College (1980).

Serving on Active Duty in the United States Army from 1959-1989, his tours include the conflict in Vietnam (1968-69); and three tours in Cold War West Germany. He completed more than 12 years as a commander of troops at the company, battalion and brigade level and authored and edited more than 1,000 magazine and newspaper articles, and nine military-related books.

An accomplished Motivational Speaker, he has delivered more than 300 presentations to soldiers, families, and civilian members of both the US and Allied nations governments. He holds numerous military distinctions and served as President Armed Forces Public Affairs Council (1987-1988). He is a Member Order of Military Medical Merit and Veterans of Foreign Wars.

Nelson L. Marsh has been preparing Federal & State Income Tax Returns since 1960. He opened his current Tax & Accounting Practice in 1986, forming his own Texas Family Closed Corporation in 1995. He is conversant in United States Taxation Law, Financial Management, Divorce Law, Adoption Law, Real Estate Law, the Law of Intent; and the greater than 80,000 pages of the Internal Revenue Code (IRS) US Code. He has setup, or assisted in creating, more than 800 Small Business Owner (SBO) organizations of all types.

Nelson L. Marsh was one of the first 200 nationwide applicants to take/pass the Registered Tax Return Preparer Test in 2011, he holds the RTRP designation from the Internal Revenue Service. He holds professional credentials as a Certified Tax Return Preparer (CRTP); Certified Individual Tax Preparer (CITP) & the annual IRS Annual Filing Tax Preparer (AFTP).

He is married to the former Anneliese Schreiweis Marsh of Stuttgart, Germany, and is the Father of three children Michele, Sharon, and Glenn, and the grandfather to his son's twin girls Annaleigh & Ellyse.

CHAPTER EXERCISE NOTES

_____

_____

_____

_____

_____

_____

_____

_____

_____

_____

_____

_____

_____

_____

_____

_____

_____

_____

_____

_____

_____

CHAPTER EXERCISE NOTES

_____

_____

_____

_____

_____

_____

_____

_____

_____

_____

_____

_____

_____

_____

_____

_____

_____

_____

_____

_____

CHAPTER EXERCISE NOTES

CHAPTER EXERCISE NOTES

_____

_____

_____

_____

_____

_____

_____

_____

_____

_____

_____

_____

_____

_____

_____

_____

_____

www.ingramcontent.com/pod-product-compliance
Lightning Source LLC
Chambersburg PA
CBHW031938190326
41519CB00007B/578